WILLIAM

CECIL RHODES

AFRICASOUTH PAPERBACKS
CAPE TOWN : JOHANNESBURG
DAVID PHILIP

AFRICASOUTH PAPERBACKS

This series includes important works of southern African literature that are at present available only in hardback or are out of print or not readily accessible or 'banned'; there is also provision for new writing. The books chosen will be not only those whose worth has become acknowledged, but also interesting and significant works that need rescue from neglect. Among the titles contracted are a number of books recently 'unbanned', after having been sent by the publisher for review. Also included in *Africasouth Paperbacks* are books from Africa south-of-the-Sahara, i.e. west, central and east African works not before available in southern Africa in paper-back, but of particular interest or needed for study purposes. The first titles available in this landmark series are listed at the back of this book.

First published 1933 by Peter Davies Ltd, London
Published 1984 in Africasouth Paperbacks by David Philip, Publisher (Pty) Ltd, 217 Werdmuller Centre, Claremont, Cape, South Africa
ISBN 0 86486 018 8
© 1984 The Literary Executor of the Estate of William Plomer

Printed by Creda Press (Pty) Ltd, Solan Road, Cape Town, South Africa

PREFACE BY GEOFFREY HARESNAPE

The broad outlines of the life of William Charles Franklyn Plomer are well known to any readers who have consulted a dictionary of literary biography. Born in the Transvaal in 1903, Plomer spent a childhood moving with his family between the United Kingdom and South Africa, and embarked upon a literary career in the Eastern Cape Province and Natal, which he was to continue in Japan and, finally, for many years in London. By the time of his death in 1973, Plomer had become a significant figure in the British literary world, and had received the honorary doctorates, the medals and other awards which came with conformity and respect. What may, however, be less known is the importance of the years from 1921 to 1926 when a young anti-establishment Plomer, resident in South Africa, subjected its society to a satiric scrutiny in cartoon, prose fiction, essay and poem. During 1925 and 1926 Plomer collaborated with Roy Campbell in the preparation and production of *Voorslag*, a magazine which hit hard at the cultural and social complacencies of the white colonialist. Both Plomer and Campbell regarded colonialism as exploitative and destructive rather than as disinterested and uplifting. In some respects they anticipate by many years the thoughts of Aimé Césaire and Frantz Fanon upon the subject. They were hostile to the heroes of the white man in Africa, be they actual historical figures like F. C. Selous or General J. C. Smuts, or mythic stereotypes such as the mining magnate, the pioneer or the Europeanised missionary. The strength of this hostility was equalled only by the strength of the sympathy which they accorded to black working-people who would have received scant attention from most whites.

Literary history reveals that *Voorslag* magazine is closely associated with a flow of literary work published between 1924 and 1934 by Plomer, Campbell, and their slightly junior associate, Laurens van der Post. Campbell confronted white colonialism not only in the pages of *Voorslag* but also in *The Wayzgoose* (1928), his bitter satire of the South Africa cultural scene, and in many of the poems collected in *Adamastor* (1930). Although Van der Post tilted at cultural narrowness in *Voorslag,* his critique of South Africa did not emerge fully until publication of *In a Province* (1934). It was Plomer who led the attack with his scintillating first novel *Turbott Wolfe* (1925), an attack which he continued in *Voorslag* and in the two collections of imaginative writing, *I Speak of Africa* and *Notes for Poems* (both 1927). The poem 'A Passage to Africa', included in the latter collection, is characteristic of his combative approach during this period. In it a young poet sails from Southampton to Cape Town on a 'liner de-luxe'. Ruthlessly he scrutinises his fellow-passengers: young women who are returning from their finishing-schools in France—'They babble French with a suburban twang / And mince their English to escape from slang'; fire-eating officers who love to reminisce about life in the trenches; culturally pretentious middle-class and middle-aged wives; and big-game hunters who are 'as fond of good clean sport as any boy'. Important targets in the young poet's attack upon colonialism are the capitalist and the missionary. 'Two brokers that talk of stocks and shares' and a dry-as-dust priest 'who plays deck-quoits with souls and cricket with emotions' are subjected to scathing criticism. The fellow-passengers deprecate the young poet's choice of the 'Colour Bar' as a topic of conversation, but he in turn perceives that their motive in going to South Africa is not their duty to protect the 'subject races', as they profess, but rather to 'have gold'. The poem ends with the young poet's triumphant realisation that he is different from all the others.

The phase of Plomer's writing—articulate, consistently developed, persistently cerebral—did not end until he had published *The Fivefold Screen* and *The Child of Queen Victoria and Other Stories* in the early 1930s. His biography of Cecil Rhodes, which appeared in 1933, should be viewed in relation to Plomer's imaginative writing of this period and against the background of the *Voorslag* movement.

Such a view of Plomer's *Cecil Rhodes* is required because the historical figure whom it concerns was not an isolated phenomenon. He was immediately identifiable with the whole entrepeneurial, culturally chauvinistic class whom Plomer and Campbell were attacking. In fact, the historical Rhodes was committed to three propositions which, to them, were anathema: (1) that the Anglo-Saxon 'race' had a duty culturally to 'uplift' Africa, (2) that a 'white' man 'worth his salt' should assiduously pursue riches (in the form of mineral wealth and real estate) on the subcontinent, and (3) that a man should be concerned in some deep, philosophical way with 'greatness'. For convenience I shall call these three propositions Cecil Rhodes's Eurocentrism, Capitalism and Titanism. Most of the books on Rhodes which appeared in the quarter century after his death in 1902 tended to back him for, and to admire, these propositions.

W. T. Stead was sensible of the 'thrill and inspiration of the mind which for less than fifty years sojourned in that tabernacle of clay'. He compared Rhodes to Alexander the Great (*The Last Will and Testament of Cecil John Rhodes*, London, 1902). For Sir Lewis Michell, Rhodes was like Clive of India: 'both were connected with the administration of Great Chartered Companies; both achieved high renown abroad and, rendered conspicuous service to their country' (*The Life of the Rt. Hon. Cecil J. Rhodes,* London, 1910).

To Ian D. Colvin he was 'honourable', 'unselfish' and 'much maligned and misunderstood' (*Cecil John Rhodes*, London, 1912). A similar implied commendation of Rhodes's three '-isms' may be found, popularised and rendered memorable in image and rhymes, in a poem by his literary protégé, Rudyard Kipling:

> Dreamer devout, by vision led
> Beyond our guess or reach,
> The travail of his spirit bred
> Cities in place of speech.
> So huge the all-mastering thought that drove —
> So brief the term allowed —
> Nations, not words, he linked to prove
> His faith before the crowd.

('The Burial — 1902')

Perhaps the only powerfully written criticism of Rhodes that was widely read during these years was Olive Schreiner's *Trooper Peter Halket of Mashonaland* (first published 1897). Her purpose in this allegory to affirm that Rhodes's Chartered Company's activities in the region of present-day Zimbabwe were exploitative and contrary to a true Christian spirit was most sympathetically regarded by Plomer and Campbell. Schreiner was, in fact, one of their great cultural heroines. For the two young poets, Rhodes could be compared to a Spanish conquistador like Cortez. In an unfinished poem of this title, Campbell clearly alludes to Rhodes's thrusts into the territory of the Ndebele and the Mashona, and to his famous parley in the Matoppos with Ndebele leaders:

> O sound the sanguinary drums
> As the North our rule extends,
> And if you do not trust your guns
> Diplomacy will gain your ends:
> Recall the fights your fathers won
> Against such odds, in such a fix —
> The rattle of the maxim-gun
> Against the clattering of sticks.
>
> ('Solo and Chorus from
>   "The Conquistador" ')

His attack, however, becomes explicit in 'The Truth about Rhodes' a satirical squib sparked off by a portrait of the magnate executed by a distinguished South African artist with whom Campbell had quarrelled over *Voorslag*:

His friends contend that Rhodes is with the saints,
His foes consign him to the Stygian shore;
But all who see him here in Roworth's paints
Will gasp for brandy and dispute no more.

(First published in *Adamastor*)

Here Campbell is counteracting Rhodes's Titanism in the same way as Cassius counteracts Caesarism in Shakespeare's play. An all-too-human fault in the 'great man' is stressed, and its possessor thereby cut down to size.

A radical deflation of Rhodes and what he stands for is also Plomer's invariable technique in his poetry and prose fiction of this period. In *Turbott Wolfe* he is satirically presented as 'the great Nigel Blades, empire-builder, the founder of our fortunes in Bladesia', a surname which, among other things, suggests the bayonet. It is this Blades who is one of the founders of 'Goldenville' where the 'Lembu', Ula Masondo, finds work and is trapped deep in a mine. During this perilous time Masondo has his surrealist dream of 'men of property' which has been evoked by his experience of Rhodesian pioneers in action: 'Sometimes these men could be seen on stoeps in the shade sipping tea and beer and blood and water; or sprawling stoutly in unbut-toned ease at gluttonous picnics; smoking pipes of leisure but not pipes of peace, while the days and hours turned over like tremendous wheels' (*I Speak of Africa*).

The pseudonymous mining city emerges in its true colours in the two 'Johannesburg' poems of *The Fivefold Screen,* and the freebooting past of many now-respectable mining-magnates and financiers is stressed:

> Riding bareback under stars
> As lordly anarchs of the veld,
> Venison feasts and tribal wars,
> Free cruelty and a cartridge belt

('Johannesburg: 1')

In his autobiography Plomer records that his father, Charles, had been sent out to South Africa in the late 1880s with a letter of introduction to Cecil Rhodes then 'in the full flush of his megalo-maniac triumph'. Plomer's account of the older man's experience contains one of the most powerful pen-portraits of Rhodes which I have read: 'The Chartered Company had an office in Capetown, and it was there that my father saw the man who was of the stuff that dictators are made of. The shy, bright-eyed boy took the chair that was offered, and *the heavy purposeful mask, with the slightly hypnotic eyes and cloven chin, leaned towards him*' (Double Lives— italics mine).

Nothing constructive came of this interview. According to Plomer, his father was too unconventional, friend-loving and easygoing to be 'worth his salt' in Rhodes's view. In later years, however, the paths of Plomer *père* and Rhodes did cross again when, as a rank-and-file member of the Bechuanaland Border Police, Charles volunteered to take part in the ill-fated Jameson Raid into the Transvaal.

When we consider that Plomer's interest in Rhodes was stimulated by personal family as well as general artistic considerations, it is not surprising that he should have turned his literary abilities to a full-scale biography. A meticulous collector and systematiser of materials, he would have had few difficulties with documentation. Rather the problem lay in what free play to allow to the imagination. He could not run the risk of mythologising Rhodes to the extent that he relaxed his grasp upon the hard facts. In a non-fictional work the satire could not be as radical as in the imaginative writing. Thus, in his introduction (p. 10) to *Cecil Rhodes* he allows that his subject possessed 'a real fame' and was 'not merely, as some have said, a vulgar land-grabber and jingo imperialist—he was what is commonly understood to be a great man'. But at the same time, he claims the right to hold an 'individual viewpoint' as to whether Rhodes was 'good', 'civilised' or 'pleasant'.

As the witty, fluent and urbane narrative unfolds, this individual viewpoint is everywhere apparent. Rhodes is taken to task for each of his three '-isms'. His Eurocentrism is seen to be suspect, partly because in Plomer's view Rhodes's notion of culture was not the best available in Great Britain, and partly because the indigenous African customs which he sought to replace were beautiful and worthwhile. For Plomer, the best tradition in English intellectual life was to be found reflected in the writings of E. M. Forster, Virginia and Leonard Woolf, Arthur Firbank and others—who valued just those qualities which Rhodes lacked: they were concerned with personal relationships; they were subtle, humorous and tolerant; and they regarded the more obvious manifestations of egotism with suspicion. Rhodes's Capitalism is viewed as an extension of egotism, and as an often ugly will to dominate. Plomer finds his larger territorial ambitions repellent, and, when pushed to an extreme, plainly absurd. He quotes with amusement Rhodes's confession to W. T. Stead: 'I would annex the planets if I could . . . I often think of that.' One of capitalism's most noxious effects in the colonial context is to compromise the innocence of missionary endeavour; for Plomer the motives of Christian ministers became dubious when they operated in the context of Rhodes's Chartered Company. Of this company's intrusion into present-day Zimbabwe he writes (p. 81):

'. . . the . . . invasion of those parts was marked by humbug and dishonesty. Lip-service was paid in London to philanthropic principles, and the crackle of rifle-fire soon broke out, like a cynical echo, in Africa. We too have our witch-doctors, and the flutter of a surplice can always be caught sight of between the machine-guns.'

Perhaps the quality with which Plomer grapples most in his biography is Rhodes's Titanism. Plomer was himself close enough to the Victorian age to be responsive to its obsessions with the absolute control of the self and of the environment. But for people of his generation the First World War had been a traumatic episode, bringing about disillusionment with Europe's fundamental cultural assumptions, a new sense of a need for social justice, and a concomitant questioning of the value of élitism. Plomer suggests that Rhodes's 'dreams' were dangerous, since they were incapable of confronting the real problems of the twentieth century. In a world which compelled countless human beings to participate in the squalor and suffering of war, the individual was at once more complex and less significant than Rhodes had imagined. For Plomer the magnate's blueprint for the ideal Rhodes Scholar seems almost ludicrous. It called for a person who would probably develop into 'a cold and truculent sahib with a thorough knowledge of ball-games and a complete ignorance of the real arts of living' (p. 170). During the course of his narrative he searches for images which will somehow do imaginative justice to the kind of man Rhodes was. One of the more sinister of these presents Rhodes as victor counting the dead bodies of African tribesmen after a skirmish near Enkeldoorn in present-day Zimbabwe: 'this heavy Semitic-looking man, wearing slightly soiled white flannel trousers and carrying a riding-crop, picking his way all alone among the beautiful corpses on that African hillside, while the groans of the wounded rose up in the incomparable freshness of the early morning air' (p. 130).

Titanism found its final expression in Rhodes's funeral provisions for his interment in the Matoppos on a mountain top which he had renamed 'The

View of the World'; for the block of granite, weighing over three tons, which, in the words of W. T. Stead, 'sealed the mouth of the sepulchre from all mortal eyes'. The pretentiousness of the event is ruthlessly undercut when Plomer writes (p. 159): 'By his own rather sentimental wish, he was buried, as is well known, in Rhodesia, in a hole in the top of a hill.'

I believe that in writing about Rhodes, Plomer came to realise that he was taking issue with a whole ruling-class ethos to which he was antipathetic. Rhodes was turning out to be just another pillar of Victorian society who had gained his weight and stature, not at home within the confines of the Establishment in church or army, but by founding himself upon the rights and territories of vulnerable peoples in southern Africa. It was perhaps inevitable that Plomer, an admirer of Bloomsbury, and himself on the list of the Hogarth Press, should in his approach to Rhodes have been influenced by Lytton Strachey's treatment of Cardinal Manning, Florence Nightingale, General Gordon and Dr. Arnold in *Eminent Victorians* (1918). Michael Herbert is surely correct to have the reservations which he expresses in 'William Plomer: A Biographical and Critical Study'* about the worth of *Cecil*

*Unpublished B. Litt. thesis, Oxford University, 1976.

Rhodes as a work of historical scholarship. As an imaginative writer Plomer made no claim to be an historian, describing the book in his introduction as a 'sketch' and wittily refusing 'to affect a gross impartiality'. Basically, he was concerned to express his intuitions regarding a figure who, in the phrase of W. T. Stead, was 'the greatest of Africanders', and who perhaps more than any other individual in the English-speaking world had given an impetus to the 'dream' of a 'white' South Africa. He found the personality upon whom that 'dream' was sustained fascinating but seriously flawed; one who both deceived others with, and was deceived by, a mystique of power and glory.

In spite of every rigour, Plomer must have found that his imagination insisted upon its own freedom. The gift for myth-making, so evident in the imaginative writing which Plomer produced in this phase of his career, may be discerned in *Cecil Rhodes* as well, although curbed by the disciplines of quotation and a very often bald prose. Underneath its patina of factual detail this biography conveys to today's reader the sense of an ogre-figure who pays for his anti-life propensities by being trapped both in the Jameson Raid debacle and in a body afflicted by an early terminal disease. Viewed in this light, *Cecil Rhodes* becomes another large piece to be fitted into Plomer's complex artistic mosaic imaging the white presence in southern Africa. To the modern historian, too, it is interesting because of the clear way, almost prophetic for its time, in which Plomer was able to perceive his subject's links with class and economic interests and with the psychology of the colonial. Paul Maylam's account of machinations and manipulations by Rhodes, and of his programmes for obtaining cheap black labour, etc. (*Rhodes, the Tswana and the British*, Westport, Connecticut, 1980) evokes an impression of the man which has more in common with Plomer's than with any other biographer's of the 1920s and 1930s. It is a pity that a writer of Plomer's sympathetic insight should have touched so lightly upon Rhodes's apparent inhibitions and that he should have refrained from exploring the possible connection between the great man's sexual psychology and his 'dreams'. But there were limits to the territory which was open even to a daring intellectual pioneer like Plomer in the early 1930s. To take the stand that he did was achievement enough.

Cape Town
March 1984

xvii

TO HUGH WALPOLE

INTRODUCTORY

CECIL RHODES was one of those men whom Nature seems to produce from time to time for the fulfilment of her own inscrutable purposes, men who seem to have about them something fatal and compelling, which makes others obey them and enables them to carry out tremendous schemes. When a man of this kind appears, all sorts of things are said to try and prove him good and wise as well as great and daemonic. But the truth may well be that the springs of action, as Lowes Dickinson once said, lie deep in ignorance and madness. Unfortunately, so much cant has been, and still is, talked about Rhodes, mainly by persons with vested interests or sluggish brains, that an earnest effort is needed to understand at all his real nature. 'Everything about him was big,' is one of the favourite catch-phrases, as though mere size were a virtue in itself. And it was of this Carnera among speculators that the Archbishop of Cape Town said in a funeral oration, 'He was not a saint in the accepted meaning of the word.' Is a fortune of millions of pounds usually got together by one man in a lifetime of no great length by means that are strictly saintly? Could irony and hypocrisy go further?

We are told that Rhodes had a deep sense of public duty, and we know that he had extraordinary tenacity of purpose. We are told that he loved mankind and lived only for their welfare. We are sure that he put the aggrandisement of his country before everything, and that he had the driving power of a monomaniac. But may we not hazard a guess that a lust for personal power largely animated this patriot? And does that man best serve his country who encourages in it, directly or indirectly, the tumescence of pride and greed and boastful self-confidence? ' In curious contrast with the lofty idealism of his aims,' says his best biographer up to the present, ' Rhodes had a strong vein of calculated cynicism in his methods.' Lofty idealism is a strange name for fanatical patriotism, and do we not judge a man by his methods? Are we not justified in assuming that a lofty idealism which is shamelessly cynical in its expression is not a lofty idealism at all? The slave of a purely worldly formula may be a very able

8

and jesuitical man, but that is not the same thing as being a lofty idealist.

In the opinion of Kruger, Rhodes was ' one of the most unscrupulous characters who have ever lived,' and this opinion was not based on mere enmity ; ' no matter how base, no matter how contemptible, be it lying, bribery or treachery, all and every means were welcome to him, if they led to the attainment of his objects.' The pot is often a good judge of the kettle's blackness.

There are no shrewder judges of character than the South African natives, and it is worth asking what was their view of the invader. They give nicknames to their white employers which often show up the nominees as in a brilliant flash of lightning. They used to call Rhodes by a name which signifies ' The Man who Separated the Fighting Bulls.' Now this is not only a heroic name, but it has about it something magical, and indeed there seemed to be something magical about Rhodes on the occasion when he earned it. Furthermore, it is recorded that he had an extraordinary influence over the natives, who are psychically sensitive, and it is said that they could never look him in the face. His high-pitched voice seemed to cast a spell over them, and it is certain that many of them looked on him as mad. From that it would follow that he was in a way sacred, and so safe from violence at their hands. The natives were right, as they often are. They recognised in him the manifestation of a natural, or perhaps even a supernatural, force ; they knew instinctively that between the slouch hat and buttoned boots there was a human dynamo.

The fame which opinion in many countries has brought into being is a real fame, and is so far standing the test of time, and the fact is plain that Rhodes was not merely, as some have said, a vulgar land-grabber and jingo imperialist—he was what is commonly understood to be a great man. Whether he is to be regarded as a good one, a really civilised one, or even a pleasant one, must depend to some extent on the individual viewpoint.

It is the purpose of this sketch neither to try and prove that Rhodes was a scoundrel, nor to affect a gross impartiality. To trace in detail the full course and implications of his financial and political life would need much greater scope than space allows or the writer possesses, but I have tried to give some slight outline of his career and beliefs, and to discover, by dealing critically with recorded facts, what kind of man this great man was. Writing about a person, I have not hesitated to be personal.

'Man never legislates,' we read in Plato, 'but destinies and accidents happening in all sorts of ways, legislate in all sorts of ways.' Bearing this in mind, we forget to cavil at Rhodes, and marvel at his career. We find ourselves abandoning all question of the supposed rightness or wrongness of his thoughts and deeds, because we feel that we are concerned with a mystery, and are brought up against problems too vast for man to solve. The more we learn of him the nearer we come to the end of all knowledge, which is a sense of overwhelming wonder and of utter ignorance.

I

CECIL JOHN RHODES was born at Bishop's Stortford on the 5th July 1853. His father, the vicar of that place, was descended from a Midland family of successful graziers and farmers, had also some Danish blood, married twice, and propagated a family of nine sons and two daughters. Cecil was the fifth son of the second wife, Louisa Peacock, whose nature was more genial than that of her husband, a man with a long nose and heavy jowl, who was strict and evangelical in his way of life. He hoped that all his sons would go into the Church, made them take Sunday-school classes and rewarded them with pious books, but as it happened, they either went into the Army or the Colonies, or both. No doubt they felt that need to escape from mid-Victorian family life which played so large a part in the expansion of the British Empire.

Cecil, described as 'a slender, delicate-looking boy of a shy nature,' was sent at the age of eight to the local grammar school. His holidays were largely spent at the house of an aunt who had married a country gentleman in a hunting district, and in a narrow, conventional world of parsons and squires he very early showed signs of being unusual. At the age of puberty, when he went out riding with some sprig of the local gentry it was noticed that he had no curiosity about girls or other individuals, but looked carefully at the acres over which he was passing, and at once appraised, with an atavistic glance, their state of cultivation or pastoral merits. This is the first indication we have of his lifelong tendency to think in terms of material things and to neglect certain claims of humanity, a tendency which found terse expression in later years in the remark, ' I prefer land to niggers,' and which obliged one of his greatest antagonists to refer to Rhodesia as ' this land where man creeps on his belly to wound his fellow in the dark, and where an acre of gold is worth a thousand souls, and a reef of shining dirt is worth half a people, and the vultures are heavy with man's flesh.'

At sixteen Cecil wanted to be a barrister, and ' next to that,' he wrote to his aunt, ' I think a clergyman's life is the nicest.' Just afterwards, however, his health broke down, and it was decided to send him out to Natal, where his brother Herbert had gone to settle. The voyage took seventy days, and he landed at Durban on the 1st October 1870. His brother, who was of a restless nature, was away at the time, and Cecil went to stay with some people at Pietermaritzburg, who found him ' very quiet and a great reader.' He had not yet given up the idea that it would be ' nice ' to be a clergyman.

His brother Herbert's farm was in the Umkomaas Valley, on the so-called South Coast of Natal, and his sojourn there helped to determine the direction of his development. It is hardly necessary to say that Umkomaas was not at that time a flourishing seaside resort. Life was very hard at first, and Herbert was trying to grow cotton on land won from the virgin bush. Sub-tropical insects, as well as the general difficulties of pioneering, were against him. But perseverance brought him some success. He was often away, and in his absence Cecil was left in charge. The younger man had to work hard, his health improved in the open air, he became self-reliant, and learnt to ' handle niggers.' Without a struggle, he became colonial in habits and sympathies, where an

immigrant of finer fibre (like Thomas Pringle
fifty years before) would have resisted. Not
that he had given up the idea of returning
to England. He had made friends with the
son of the local magistrate, and the two
young men resolved to ' keep up their classics.'
Rhodes had quite made up his mind to go
sooner or later to Oxford, for he saw that real
benefit might be had from taking such a step,
and he believed, as he put it later, that ' the
Oxford system in its most finished form *looks*
very unpractical, yet, wherever you turn your
eye—except in science—an Oxford man is at
the top of the tree.'

Rhodes had only been three months in the
Umkomaas district when his brother Herbert
departed for the recently discovered Diamond
Fields, leaving Cecil in sole charge of the
cotton farm. A more peaceful man might
have been content to spend the rest of his life
at Umkomaas, which had then the makings
of an earthly paradise. The climate is excellent, the soil is fertile, a mild breeze blows
in from the Indian Ocean, the blossoming
branches of the coral-tree are reflected in the
river, many fruits ripen, and the grasshopper's
note helps to produce an atmosphere of drowsy
calm. But the Rhodes brothers were not men

of peace, and a year after his arrival Cecil disposed of the farm and went to join Herbert, who was having some success in the search for diamonds. He made the immense journey across the veld in a scotch-cart drawn by a team of oxen, and carried with him a pick, two spades, several volumes of those classics which he had resolved to 'keep up,' and a Greek lexicon.

Kimberley was in those days a scene of feverish activity, and the local colour was somewhat Bret Hartean. Fortune-hunters of all kinds arrived in a steady stream, many from the slums of Europe. It was not unusual for as many as thirty waggon-loads of new-comers to arrive in one day, and at New Rush there was soon a collection of forty thousand people, all living under tents or corrugated iron, amid heaps of gravel, clouds of dust, and a variety of smells. 'The dust of the dry diggings,' said an eye-witness, 'is to be classed with plague, pestilence and famine, and if there is anything worse, with that also.' The price of necessaries was very high, and water cost threepence a bucket. In Rhodes's own words, the place looked 'like an immense number of ant-heaps covered with black ants, as thick as can be, the latter represented by human beings.' Many of the diggers, however, were at least picturesque, being ' dressed in corduroy or shoddy, high-booted, bare as to arms and breast, with beard of any length, girt with a butcher's knife on a belt of leather.'

Colesberg Kopje, the hill which was the scene of New Rush, soon disappeared, boulders and all, a sacrifice to the shovels of the diggers, and in its place was a crater, increasing in size every minute. Round the edge of this crater a timber framework or scaffolding had to be built, tier below tier, and on the narrow floors thus improvised winches were rigged up with ropes passing inward and down to the claims below. The bottom of the mine, an uneven checkerwork of claims, was thus criss-crossed by innumerable ropes which formed a vast web above the diggers. The gangs below loaded the buckets, while those above turned the winches. As the buckets appeared at the top they were passed on to the pounders and sorters who worked at tables in the open air. The rough work was, of course, done by natives, the owners supervising and sorting at the tables.

On the edge of this remarkable chasm sat a tall, fair boy, blue-eyed, with aquiline features, slightly Hebraic and distinctly predatory. He

17

was sitting at a table and sorting diamonds, and he kept a sharp look-out to see that no native should slip a diamond into his mouth or any other personal recess. Altogether there was a great deal to do. There were claims to look after, natives to control, deals to be done, and he had to hold his own among the riff-raff. He appeared moody and preoccupied, and 'hardly ever had a companion'; but it was soon clear that he had the makings in him of a very capable business man.

Of course a mining-camp has its pleasures. But it was quite a mistake to suppose, Herbert wrote home, that there were no 'nice girls' in Kimberley. There were dance-halls, too, but when the handsome Cecil entered them it was only 'for exercise.' In fact, says a contemporary, 'I do not believe if a flock of the most adorable women passed through the street, he would go across the road to see them.'

Before two years had passed, the brothers had prospered. The highveld air, in spite of dust and germs, had restored Cecil's health, and as there was some ready money in hand, he returned to England and matriculated at Oriel, keeping the Michaelmas term in 1873. It was not long, however, before he caught a chill at rowing. His heart and lungs were affected, and the specialist who saw him ordered him back to Africa, writing in his case-book, ' Not six months to live.' In its own way, Rhodes's heart was almost as significant an organ as Cleopatra's nose. Had it been weaker—or stronger—the whole aspect of Africa would have been altered. But Kimberley made it throb with eagerness—there was profitable business to be done.

Rhodes went into partnership with one Rudd, a man much older than himself, and together they increased their holdings, especially in De Beers. He was soon recognised as the ablest speculator in the district with the exception of Barney Barnato, who, as Barnet Isaacs, had been not very long before ' a little, weakly, sorrowful child sitting crying on a doorstep in Middlesex Street ' ; who had come out to Africa with a capital of £30 and forty boxes of doubtful cigars ; and who was now a ' kopje-walloper,' or casual diamond-buyer, full of ' the false bonhomie of the street corner.' And at this time Rhodes was helped in speculation by Alfred Beit, a shrewd but timorous Hamburg Jew, who had, unlike so many, come to Kimberley with capital behind him.

The relationship between Rhodes and Beit was destined to last, and to be of such importance that General Smuts thinks that, without Beit, Rhodes might have been ' a mere political visionary, bereft of power of practical creation.' Nobody recognised more clearly than Beit himself that he was a better business man than Rhodes, who was not a good bargainer and too eager to get a deal quickly settled. Also Rhodes, owing partly to a certain lack of interest in individuals, was sometimes taken in by them, whereas Beit's judgment of men is said to have been ' positively uncanny.' His judgment of Rhodes was mingled with a perhaps peculiarly Jewish kind of hero-worship. He admired Rhodes both for being so like and so unlike himself. The little man looked up to the six-foot commercial Viking and marvelled at his boldness and Oxonian interludes ; the Jew admired the Jewishness in Rhodes's character. In putting his money on Rhodes, Beit certainly backed a winner. So much did he admire his hero that he took eagerly to Rhodes's politics and became, in his Park Lane snuggery, more English than the English. He was content in later years to be a power behind the bludgeon, and to know that Rhodes would solve a financial difficulty by the formula, ' Ask little Alfred.'

It was no doubt from Beit that Rhodes learnt two of the most useful of business axioms—that men will often admire you and follow you like a dog because you have encouraged them to think that you trust them ; and that a name for generosity is an excellent advertisement. Beit, as his biographer, Mr. Seymour Fort, is careful to point out, knew ' the value of generosity in business,' and, as a matter of policy, ' never refused to help a " lame duck." ' It has often been said that Rhodes helped people freely with money, and so he did. But why, when a very rich man is able to buy support, he should be considered virtuous for quite cynically doing so, can only be explained by the common human wish to think a great man good.

II

KIMBERLEY was no bed of roses. The tall and dusty young man, wearing trousers that had once been white, and brooding over his thoughts, had plenty of troubles. Kimberley was the scene of recurring difficulties—disease and fever from bad drains and living conditions, droughts and floods, jealousies and intrigues, taxation, litigation and crime. Many of the diggers left, but Rhodes stayed on. He wanted to obtain power by amalgamating as many interests as possible, and Barnato provided the stimulus of rivalry. In Kimberley Rhodes had become a person of some consequence, and it was in Kimberley that he meant to retain and improve his position. At the age of twenty-three he was able to control ' a body of angry men ' at a Board meeting, and it was clear to everybody that he had not only a future, but a present.

He found time, however, to spend eight months in a solitary journey by ox-waggon through Bechuanaland and the Transvaal, a journey which took him through miles and miles of healthy country with all sorts of farming and mining possibilities, and brought him into close contact with the Dutch. The fresh air did his health so much good that he was able to return to Oxford and for several years led an unusual double life between the university and the mine, where his long vacations were spent.

At Oxford he is said to have belonged to ' a set which lived a good deal apart from both games and work,' and to have been much younger in manner than the other undergraduates, who ' were full of that spurious wisdom assumed by many young men as a defensive armour, an armour he did not require.' There was a real determination in his continuance of his Oxford career. He had made up his mind to go through with it, and when Rhodes had thoroughly made up his mind about anything he was like an elemental force, like a stream of water which progresses through, round or over any objects which it cannot sweep before it.

He did not escape the influence of Ruskin, which was making itself felt at Oxford in those days. That Rhodes's creed, when formed, resulted from the culmination in him of the whole tendency of the age towards expansion may well be true, and it should be remembered that in England people were busy trying to justify that expansion in a variety of high-flown terms, religious and otherwise. Ruskin himself was preaching in such terms as these : ' This is what England must either do, or perish : she must found colonies as fast and as far as she is able, formed of her most energetic and worthiest men ; seizing every piece of fruitful waste ground she can set her foot on, and there teaching these her colonists . . . that their first aim is to be to advance the power of England by land and sea. . . . All that I ask of you is to have a fixed purpose of some kind for your country and for yourselves, no matter how restricted, so that it be fixed and unselfish.' Added to this influence was that of Winwood Reade's *Martyrdom of Man*, a book which Rhodes is known to have read and admired, and which preaches that man must use his own powers and not expect aid from non-existing supernatural powers.

At the age of twenty-four the young man had his first bad heart attack. It brought home to him some sense of the precariousness of life and of the necessity for getting on with whatever he was going to do. It made him thought-

ful and helped him to formulate the ' cause '
he was to live for. How remarkable that cause
was may be gathered from the first of his
series of wills. This will is dated 19th September 1877, and the testator leaves the fortune he has not yet made for ' the establishment, promotion and development of a Secret
Society the aim and object whereof shall be
the extension of British rule throughout the
world, the perfecting of a system of emigration from the United Kingdom and of colonisation by British subjects of all lands where the
means of livelihood are attainable by energy,
labour and enterprise, and especially the
occupation by British settlers of the entire
continent of Africa, the Holy Land, the valley
of the Euphrates, the islands of Cyprus and
Candia, the whole of South America, the
islands of the Pacific not heretofore possessed
by Great Britain, the whole of the Malay
Archipelago, the sea-board of China and
Japan, the ultimate recovery of the United
States of America as an integral part of the
British Empire, the inauguration of a system
of colonial representation in the Imperial Parliament, which may tend to weld together the
disjointed members of the Empire, and finally
the foundation of so great a power as here-

after to render wars impossible and promote the best interests of humanity.'

This project was described by W. T. Stead as ' the idea which dominated Mr. Rhodes's imagination,' and he went on to say that his friend ' aimed at the foundation of a society composed of men of strong convictions and of great wealth, which would do for the unity of the English-speaking race what the Society of Jesus did for the Catholic Church immediately after the Reformation. The English-speaking race stood to Mr. Rhodes for all that the Catholic Church stood to Ignatius Loyola.' It is important to realise that these ideas, which may be taken as those of an enthusiast or a fanatic, according to taste, were the ones which mainly governed the course of Rhodes's life. We have it on Jameson's authority that even at that early period Rhodes ' had mapped out his whole policy just as it has since been developed.' The policy was modified by necessity, not by intellectual growth, and after the lapse of many years, during which Rhodes had fought all kinds of enemies in Africa by flaunting the Union Jack in their faces, or had won them over by his persuasiveness, perhaps the only change was that he expressed ' an unhesitating readiness to accept the reunion of the race under the Stars and Stripes if it could not be obtained in any other way.'

Rhodes was not unconscious of his role as a man of destiny, and he regarded his ' idea ' as one ' requiring the devotion of the best souls of the next 200 years.' It does not seem to have occurred to him that many of the ' best souls ' at any given moment might not be of the English-speaking race and might not be especially keen on the advancement of that race, nor that many of the ' best souls ' of our own race might have little interest in trying to dominate mankind by means of a sort of glorified Ku-Klux Klan. No, the ' best souls ' seem to have many other kinds of fish to fry.

It is by his ' idea ' that Rhodes stands or falls in the individual estimation, and his obsession with it will seem to justify, or fail to justify, his career. If we believe in the Empire, if we believe that the English-speaking peoples really can show the world the best way to live, if we believe that the extension and maintenance of the *pax Britannica* is the best means of trying to induce people of the most various races to behave fairly reasonably, and that they either can or ought to be so induced, then we may be ready to overlook Rhodes's crudenesses and admire him more or less wholeheartedly for his efforts to promote his cause.

In religion he was scarcely a Christian (he had ' concluded on a fifty per cent. chance that there was a God ') ; in thought and politics he had none of the restraint of the true Conservative ; in economics he was a thorough-going capitalist. There are many people to-day who find it hard to sympathise with that woolly kind of ' religion ' which encourages chatter about ' God's purpose ' for ' His Anglo-Saxon race ' and ' bringing nearer the reign of justice and liberty,' and who have profound doubts about capitalism and that attitude of mind which is apt to lead to a firm belief in one's own superiority and enlightenment, and to a continual interference, in the name of ' liberty,' with other people. To such as these Rhodes will seem a somewhat suspect hero. They will not be able to help marvelling at the energy with which he fulfilled his destiny, but apart, let us hope, from a vain attempt to fix individual blame too closely, they will retain a regret that the South African natives should have been deprived of their land and their communal system without getting a decent alternative in exchange ; that the South

African Dutch should have been so much brow-beaten and hindered in their efforts to make a little world of their own ; and that on the veld Mammon should have been persistently worshipped as God—as if spiritual drought were necessary to match the dryness of the soil.

III

BEFORE he was thirty, he took the important step of entering South African politics. When Griqualand West, which contained the Diamond Fields, was absorbed into the Cape Colony, two electoral divisions were formed : Rhodes was returned for one of them, and held the seat for the rest of his life. But before concentrating his entire attention on South African matters this extraordinary person returned to Oxford, and, already a financier and member of the Cape Parliament, at last took his degree. Financier, politician, and alumnus, they were all subservient to the dreamer, who had now taken command and was vigorously pointing northwards. Rhodes soon made it clear that his aim was, as we have seen, to extend and confirm the area and force of British settlement and influence, especially in Africa, and to promote generally what might be called, in present-day jargon, Empire-mindedness. But Majuba had just been fought, and Rhodes was not alone in feeling that Gladstone's recognition of the Transvaal Republic was a 'surrender.' In fact, his mood is said to have been one of 'unspeakable anger.'

His principal rival in Cape politics was Jan Hofmeyr, who was also a believer in nationalism—but Dutch nationalism—and in a federation of the various South African states. Hofmeyr was essentially a man of moderate views, who believed in co-operation between the English and Dutch, and it soon became clear that he and Rhodes were not widely divergent in their views on the desirability of unity, and in time they became good friends. Federation, however, was less Rhodes's immediate concern than expansion. 'The Boers,' Livingstone had said, 'resolved to shut up the interior and I determined to open the country.' Rhodes followed Livingstone, and concentrated upon the problem of securing a free corridor to the north, to the vast interior. The corridor was Bechuanaland. 'I look upon this Bechuanaland territory,' he said in a speech, 'as the Suez Canal of the trade of this country, the key of its road to the interior.' And in a later speech he described it as 'the neck of the bottle.' It commanded the route to the Zambesi. 'We must secure it,' he insisted, 'unless we are prepared to see the whole of the north pass out of our hands.' Into whose hands? That was the question.

The situation in Bechuanaland was in every way complicated. Various white adventurers had taken advantage of disputes between the native chiefs to get hold of land, and Boer trekkers from the Transvaal had already established the two tiny republics of Stellaland and the Land of Goshen right across the road to the interior. Rhodes was most anxious to keep the way clear, and he felt that there was no time to be lost. But his appeals to the Cape Parliament were not well received, and few people seemed to care about the possibility that the Transvaal might annex the lands in question. At this critical moment, however, circumstances aided him unexpectedly. The scramble for Africa was already well under way, and the Germans became a new menace to his ' dreams.' Bismarck, at first reluctant to encourage German colonisation (he had expressly denied ' the least design to establish any footing in South Africa '), now changed his tune, and early in 1884 announced a German protectorate over Damaraland and Namaqualand, a vast territory more than 300,000 square miles in extent. The indifference and the dividedness of both the Imperial and Colonial Governments had been taken advantage of, and the ' bottle neck ' was in danger of being corked up. Rhodes, besides bringing others round to his views, had managed to win the ear of the High Commissioner, Sir Hercules Robinson, and as a result of firm representations in London a protectorate, after endless complications, was declared.

Confusion, however, was to mark the Bechuanaland question for some time to come. It was given no small impetus by the appointment of John Mackenzie as resident deputy-commissioner. This individual, a missionary of considerable experience, held strong convictions. A contentious Scotchman with a good opinion of himself, he was fond of the natives (who called him *Tau*, the Lion), hated the Dutch for oppressing them, and was a zealous Imperialist. Of his sincerity there is no doubt, but Nature did not intend him for a diplomat. His tactlessness appears to have been of the aggressive kind, and his faculty for doing the wrong thing (wrong, that is, in a political sense) positively automatic. He seems to have made it fairly plain to the Dutch that he thought them a pack of rascals and meant to treat them accordingly, and is accused of having openly tried to sow discord among them, and of having countenanced native attacks upon them. After setting everybody more at loggerheads than before, he raised the Union Jack with a flourish and demanded a large police force to support his authority. And yet the historians have not perhaps been quite fair to him, probably because the active creature's good intentions were negrophilist rather than commercial. He was backed by the Aborigines Protection Society, he had a strong feeling that the natives were more likely to get a fair deal if they came directly under Crown and not (as Rhodes desired) Cape control, and he continued to work for them and to oppose to the best of his ability the violent invasion of the interior by the needy and greedy, the shoals of land sharks and shady sahibs, whose advance was eventually made so much easier by the strong current of Rhodes's monomania. Mackenzie was no disbeliever in the merits of his own race and its right to assert itself. In fact, he behaved for the most part as if the Great White Queen was at his very elbow. He was a man with knowledge of the country and its inhabitants, and was by no means without ideas, and if the

history of the establishment of the Bechuanaland protectorate was not such a tangle of
cross-purposes, such a chronicle of squabbles,
such a nightmare of 'muddling through,'
which would probably be as tedious to revive
as it is saddening to learn about, it might be
worth while to reconsider the whole matter
of Mackenzie *versus* Rhodes. It certainly
appears that Rhodes lost no chance of under-
mining Mackenzie's authority by belittling
his efforts and upsetting his policy. He may
simply have seen in him an obstacle in the
way of fulfilling his 'dreams,' but it looks very
much as though his love of power made him
jealous. He managed, at all events, to oust
him.

Sir Hercules Robinson, on the pretext of
wishing to confer with Mackenzie, recalled
him and sent Rhodes (who had just refused an
invitation from General Gordon to the Sudan)
to replace him in Bechuanaland. Robinson
considered that that country was probably
already lost to the Dutch, gave Rhodes no
definite instructions, and while allowing him
a free hand, cautioned him, saying, 'If you
get into a mess I cannot back you up.' With
the directness of genius Rhodes went straight
to the point. Van Niekerk, the Administrator

of Stellaland, was then encamped with a supporting commando from the Transvaal. In the presence of a hostile armed force Rhodes showed no fear. He found himself face to face with Van Niekerk's chief lieutenant, a person known as 'Groot' Adriaan de la Rey, 'a huge uncouth Boer from the backveld with a sinister reputation for violence,' and more than once a brutal murderer. When he spoke to de la Rey, he received the ogreish reply, 'Blood must flow.' 'No,' said Rhodes, 'give me my breakfast first, and we can talk about blood afterwards.' This was superb. The fearsome Goliath had been conquered by a few words in which common sense and coolness were mingled with charm, and before the week was out Rhodes had become godfather to the ogre's grandchild. It was not the only occasion in his life on which, having taken a bull by the horns, he first patted it on the head, and then taught it to eat out of his hand. A settlement was made between Rhodes and Van Niekerk, stipulating that the British protectorate must be recognised, but repudiating all Mackenzie's proceedings, and most tactfully allowing that the land-titles of the Stellaland farmers should be recognised officially.

With the Goshenites Rhodes was less successful, and when Kruger violated the recently signed London Convention by interfering, it was felt that it was time to teach both the Transvaal and the Germans a lesson. An expeditionary force under Sir Charles Warren was therefore sent to ' pacify ' the country and to hold it until a further policy had been decided upon. One of Warren's first acts was to arrange a meeting with Kruger at Fourteen Streams. He was accompanied by both Mackenzie and Rhodes, and it was on this occasion that Kruger is supposed to have said of the latter, ' That young man will cause me trouble if he does not leave politics alone and turn to something else. Well, the racehorse is swifter than the ox, but the ox can draw the greater loads. We shall see.'

Rhodes differed so much from Warren and Mackenzie, who between them helped to bungle matters considerably, that he felt bound to resign and leave Bechuanaland. But it had been made clear to the world, and to Germany and the Transvaal in particular, that England was going to keep the corridor to the interior. One of Rhodes's ' dreams ' had, largely by his own efforts, come true.

While busy in Bechuanaland or at Cape

Town, he had not lost sight of his business interests. The De Beers Company, for example, had increased its capital fourfold in the course of a few years. But in 1886 there was much ado about the discovery of gold on the Witwatersrand. To a burgher who gleefully brought him news of it General Joubert prophetically replied, 'Instead of rejoicing you would do better to weep; for this gold will cause our country to be soaked in blood.' If Rhodes had been able to take full advantage of the chance that offered, there might have been scarcely a limit to his wealth and power. It is a disturbing thought, because history does not encourage the idea that human beings are particularly fitted to be autocrats; it is also a reflection on the haphazard economic system which allows of such a possibility.

Opportunity has seldom knocked at anyone's door with such a sledge-hammer, and such a golden one at that, but when Rhodes reached the Rand he was to some extent misled by the opinions of experts who told him that the reef would come to little. He would not at first commit himself. 'It's all very well,' he said to Dr. Hans Sauer, who was trying to persuade him to buy some land, 'but I cannot calculate the power in these claims.' His choice of the word *power* is curiously characteristic—it was evidently a synonym for gold. He did very early acquire considerable holdings, which were taken over by the Consolidated Gold Fields Company, and became a gold magnate, if not the dictator he was to become in Kimberley.

Besides the warnings of the experts and his own doubts, there was another circumstance which prevented Rhodes from getting every possible iron into the fire. For some time he had been on very intimate terms with one Neville Pickering, who was described as ' a frank, sunny-tempered young Englishman.' The two were almost inseparable. They ' shared the same office and the same dwelling-house ' in Kimberley. They ' worked together and played together.' They had also been in the habit of riding together, and on one occasion, two years before this time, Pickering had been violently thrown by his horse. He had never got over the accident. Indeed, it had affected his lungs, and his health had gradually given way. By the time Rhodes had left for the Rand, his friend was already in a decline.

And now Dr. Sauer had secured options which might have made Rhodes nearly all-powerful in Johannesburg. He had obtained, for example, an option for £500 on a farm where afterwards more than twenty million pounds' worth of gold was mined. The negotiations were complete, the deeds of transfer were ready for the signature of the unusually hesitant Rhodes, when something happened which made him reach a quick decision—but not the decision that was being urged upon him. A message came from Kimberley to say that Pickering could not live much longer. Rhodes turned to Sauer and said, ' I'm off.' There was no vacant place in the mail-cart, so he made the journey seated on the mail-bags which were roped on the top of it. It was springtime on the veld.

The frantic Sauer telegraphed again and again to Kimberley without result, and the options lapsed which might have made Rhodes absolute master of the world's chief source of gold. It was as if fate itself had intervened, and had made Rhodes for once obey his heart instead of his pocket, as though to limit the power that might be exercised by one man alone. Fate, however, must have been a little half-hearted, for after six years the capital of the Gold Fields Company had been increased by a million and a quarter; by 1895 the dividend was no less than fifty per cent. ; Rhodes himself for several years drew from the Company an income of between £300,000 and £400,000 ; and this helped eventually to bring his total yearly income up to at least a million.

However, to his great credit, he did leave the Rand for Pickering. Pickering was mortally ill, and Rhodes would not leave his bedside. Finally, on the 16th October, the young man whispered, 'You have been father, mother, brother and sister to me,' and died in Rhodes's arms.

IV

Nothing in his life is more distinguished than his devotion to the dying Pickering. It is an indication that his worship of Mammon was liable to a sudden breakdown—unless we are cynical enough to conclude that he thought Pickering, simply as a servant of his 'dreams,' as a potentially valuable lieutenant, in need of personal succour. There seems to be some reason to think that the shock of losing this young man who had so enchanted him was an emotional one, and it may possibly have had something to do with his tendency to cultivate more and more a hardness and even brutality of manner which, it was supposed by some, was not really natural to him but served to hide his susceptibilities.

No woman seems ever to have been as dear to him as Pickering was. Commonly spoken of as a woman-hater, Rhodes was very shy in the presence of women, and they often made him blush. He seems to have had a boyish respect for them and little interest in their charms. ' It was foreign to his nature when in ladies' company to employ ambiguous or equivocal language, or any term or insinuation which might have the effect of embarrassing a delicate and refined mind,' says one of his intimates with much ingenuousness. When Rhodes admired women, it was not so much for their beauty as for their brains or character or tact. He often ran away from them in self-defence, and when asked why he did not marry, he ' appeared quite shy ' and said that he was too busy to get married, and would not be able to do his duty as a husband towards his wife. Whatever he may have meant by that, he advanced the lame excuse that he would be much absent from home. A man who knew him remarked that his ' imperviousness to the sex in general ' was a source of strength in that it would protect him from ' the seductive wiles of a diplomatic Delilah.' There was at least one not very diplomatic Delilah who did her best with him in later years, as will appear.

Few men or women could resist him. ' In-difference,' said his most persistent female admirer, ' was impossible towards this strange being who, with all his vices, the arrogance, the overbearing insolence of the race to which he belonged, possessed also an uncommon attractiveness which drew towards him even his most passionate detractors.' He had that charm of manner which is often found in exceptional people who know what they want of life, and in people working absorbedly for a ' cause.' The hold over others which is obtained by such men is partly due to the atmosphere of certainty which surrounds them. Most men, as Rhodes himself once said, are either fools or weathercocks. Most men crave, in this uncertain world, for what is definite, cut-and-dried, in belief and behaviour. And this is no doubt why a man who really knows what he wants so often gets it, or at least a part of it. ' I have found out one thing,' he once said, ' and that is, if you have an idea and it is a good idea, if you will only stick to it, you will come out all right.' Such a man compels the help of many of those who have no minds to make up, or minds that are made up afresh as often as the wind or—what comes to the same thing to-day—the propaganda of the Press barons changes. To realise how little limit there is to the power that is generated now and then in individuals who believe passionately in a single and ruthlessly simple political idea, we have only to think of such

44

different figures in our own day as Lenin, Mussolini and Hitler.

So compelling was Rhodes's very manner that a hard-boiled business man would approach him in a hostile mood, would soon be in agreement with him, and would leave him convinced that the two of them had really been at one in their views all the time. And it is significant that whenever really able people encountered him they at once recognised his power. General Gordon, with whom he served in the Basutoland enquiry of 1882, in asking for his co-operation elsewhere, said, ' There are few men in the world to whom I would make such an offer, but of course you will have your own way. I never met a man so strong for his own opinion ; you think your views are always right.' He was not really a good speaker, and by no means always a good talker, would labour a point that others took for granted, would utter clumsy platitudes in the belief that they were epigrams, but somehow when ' the rapid sentences poured out of the broad chest in curiously high notes that occasionally rose to a falsetto,' English people, Dutch people, black people, election audiences, business rivals, and High Commissioners were all in danger of going down like ninepins. People said he was not much of a horseman, they found him a poor hand at bridge and billiards, he was domineering and irritable, but nobody could deny that he was wonderful.

His 'private and confidential' secretaries, who had the closest and most continuous contact with him, twinkled in the reflected glory of the planet of which they were the satellites. One of them, after a first casual meeting with Rhodes, could think of nothing but the delight of being employed by him, although not a word had been said about it. 'I would lie awake half the night,' he has confessed, 'working myself up into a state of delirious excitement, speculating on the joy and pleasure which would be mine when I should be his secretary. . . . I had an intense desire to work for him and to please him.' Another explicitly remarks that 'whether Rhodes liked women or not, he did prefer the society of men.' He preferred the society of colonials, younger than himself, and of course much inferior in ability. He liked to have about him a 'sort of bodyguard of young men in whom he was interested,' and one of them has told us that they were 'much more companions than secretaries in the ordinary sense of the word.' The fact

46

is, Rhodes liked to be with people who would put up with his uncertain temper and clumsy jokes, people whom he could order about, and who would be attached to him in a boyish sort of way, looking up to him as somebody wonderful, and not interfering with his ambitious thoughts or his self-assurance. And although the ideas which dominated him were few and simple, these young men were ' lost without him.' He had a real gift for getting subordinates to do his work, and in doing their share the friends and companion-secretaries, from Jameson down, felt proud and honoured, speaking of him as ' the Old Man '—a nickname which was used for Rhodes even by some of his elders when he was still quite young.

Nobody, it seems, ever quite took the place of Pickering, but in later years the favourite was one Jack Grimmer, originally a junior clerk in De Beers, known as one of ' Rhodes's lambs,' *i.e.* one of about a dozen young men who went up country with Rhodes from Kimberley in the early days. Grimmer was a stolid being who thought Plato was ' a lot of damned rot,' and treated Rhodes like ' a great baby.' Rhodes used to say that Grimmer's demeanour had a restful and soothing effect on him. When he was ill he always wanted Grimmer to be with him, and he is said to have shown great pleasure in this man's companionship. When Grimmer was ill from a scorpion bite at Inyanga in 1897, Rhodes was greatly concerned and sat with him all day; and shortly afterwards, when Grimmer was down with fever, Rhodes used to sit by him with a basin of vinegar and bathe his feet, in the fond hope that this would cure him.

Anyone who wishes to speak of Rhodes's private life has to avoid on the one hand the reticence or cant of his biographers, and on the other the looseness or falsehood of scandal. Any man who makes a forceful move in the world is bound to stir up clouds of busy-tongued nonentities, particularly in his immediate neighbourhood—just as a stallion breaking loose from its stable and galloping off to light and liberty will leave behind it a peevish buzzing of flies—and in South Africa there have always been plenty of stories, some highly coloured, about Rhodes's self-indulgences, stories often springing from the frustrated desires of their originators. Rhodes was inclined to be a gross feeder, and had he been a little less carnivorous he might possibly have been a milder man. With regard to drink, it is obvious that no drunkard could have accomplished half as much as Rhodes did in his comparatively short span of life. People drank more in those days than they do now ; South Africa, in some ways a frightful country—' Fancy,' said Olive Schreiner, ' a whole nation of *lower* middle-class Philistines ! '—has made many a good man take to drink ; and Rhodes, owing to the state of his heart and the efforts of his brain and nervous system, was obviously in a position to benefit by some use of stimulants. That he chose, like Bismarck, to drink a mixture of stout and champagne at eleven in the morning is surely a matter for regret rather than condemnation. So far from Rhodes's taste for alcohol being a fearful vice, it was one of his more pleasant traits, and no doubt a very helpful one. He was drunk for years on end—but it was with power, that fiercest of intoxicants.

V

RETURNING from Johannesburg to Kimberley, Rhodes applied himself to the solution of a problem which had long occupied his attention—the amalgamation of the various diamond interests into one concern under his own control. The idea that amalgamation was necessary had, of course, occurred to others besides himself—indeed, the numerous cross-tunnellings in progress were causing constant encroachments and disputes—but no one else was able to bring such determination to bear upon it. His business ability, his good management and up-to-date machinery, had enabled him, in the course of a few years, to reduce the costs of production by more than half. He had also managed to stop heavy losses which had been incurred by the native employees' habit of selling diamonds on the sly to the so-called 'illicit' diamond buyers. The leakage was now remedied by keeping the natives shut up in compounds where they could be most rigorously searched for diamonds, as if for lice. Here, too, they were provided with ginger-beer in order that their efficiency might not be impaired, as it had been formerly, by over-indulgence in the pleasures of alcohol. In spite of this commercial triumph, however, a new danger arose, of a kind common enough in the history of industry—the danger of over-production.

The world's demand for diamonds was considered to be limited, and now here were Barney Barnato's group, besides a French Company, and Rhodes's De Beers as well, producing more and more diamonds, of which the price was already tending to sink. Steps obviously had to be taken to keep their value up to that artificial level at which these coveted pebbles have since remained. Barnato thought the best way of overcoming the difficulty was by a working agreement between the various interests which would check wasteful competition and give him time to increase his own power. But Rhodes, with his usual directness, at once went to the heart of the matter, and then, as the tolerant Mr. Basil Williams puts it, ' began a rare game of beggar-my-neighbour '—a game that has justly been described elsewhere in somewhat harsher terms. ' The special type of instinct which Providence had implanted in Mr. Cecil Rhodes,' says Lord Olivier, ' unerringly inspired him to discern that a monopoly of the supply of the finest diamonds was the most auspicious and appropriate foundation imaginable for a policy of commercial Imperialism. . . . He succeeded by irrepressible energy, cajolery, perseverance and unscrupulousness in amalgamating the principal interests in the diamond diggings, and established De Beers.'

Rhodes's first step was to leave for Europe, where, with the support of Lord Rothschild, he managed to buy out the French interest for £1,400,000. But the agreement with the French directors had still to be confirmed by the shareholders, and before that happened Barnato had offered a much larger sum. Rhodes then went to Barnato with his business acumen, or cunning, hidden under a mask of frankness. It would be a pity, he said, for them to waste money in cutting each other's throats, and he offered Barnato the French Company in exchange for the equivalent of the purchase price in Barnato shares. Barnato accepted the offer, thus giving Rhodes one-fifth of the capital of his own Kimberley Central mine—he forgot that one needs a long spoon to sup with the Devil. He imagined that he would still be able to retain control, but Rhodes, having obtained so firm a footing, determined to get what he called ' the whip-hand.' Rhodes found he would need £2,000,000 for the purpose, and said to Beit, his little Jewish henchman, ' Where's the money to come from ? ' ' Oh, we'll get the money,' answered Beit, ' if we can only buy the shares.' They bought the shares, they found the money, and Rhodes became supreme in the diamond industry.

Rhodes's triumph and Barnato's climbdown was celebrated by a curiously degraded exchange of courtesies. Snobbery, it seems, prevails even in a mining-camp. An institution called the Kimberley Club had not opened its doors to Barnato, who was sufficiently poor-spirited to beg Rhodes to take him to lunch there. When this pathetic social ambition had been gratified, Rhodes asked of Barnato a favour in return. He wanted, he said, to see something he had never yet seen—a bucketful of diamonds. When Barnato produced it, Rhodes plunged his hands into it, and gloated over the stones as they ran through his fingers. Another ' dream ' had come true.

It need hardly be added that the establishment of the monopoly brought distress to many private individuals who were not dominated so much by greed and ambition as by the immediate need to make a living ; they could no longer even sell goods to the native workmen, for the monopoly took care to do that henceforth, making, we may be sure, a cosy profit in the process. When it came to drawing up the trust deed for the united De Beers Company, Rhodes made it quite plain that he wanted the Company to be a political instrument. He was opposed by Barnato, whom, after a talk lasting nearly twenty-four hours, he browbeat into submission. ' I want it put in the trust deed,' he said, ' that we have the power to go to the Zambesi, or further north, to spend the money of the company, if thought advisable, to acquire a country and form an empire.' It thus became clear that the whole business of amalgamation had simply been a step in the direction of realising his ' dreams.' He had his way over the De Beers trust deed, and when it was drawn up it was seen that no Company since the East India Company had had such power. As a legal authority pointed out, the Company was not confined to Africa ; it was authorised to take steps for the government of any country ; and, if it obtained a charter in accordance with the trust deed from the Secretary of State, it could annex territory in Central Africa, raise and maintain a standing army, and make war. Of this corporation Rhodes, at the age of thirty-six, was the head.

' We must always remember,' he said again, harping on his one perennial string, ' that the gist of the South African question lies in the extension of the Cape Colony to the Zambesi.' Others might consider that it lay more probably in the future relationships between the races, between English and Dutch, and more especially between white and black. But Rhodes had at this time particular reason for apprehension about the north, and the source of that apprehension did not now lie in Bechuanaland. Reports were reaching him that Kruger had turned his attention to the vast hinterland that lay beyond the Transvaal. Not only had Boer hunters been active in that region, but the Germans, now established in South-West Africa, were not unaware of its existence, and the Portuguese had actually issued an official map marking it as their own.

The country in question was known as Matabeleland. The Matabele, an offshoot of the Zulus, had begun trekking at about the time when the Voortrekkers were leaving the Cape, that is to say, in the eighteen-thirties. Coming into conflict with the Basuto and the Dutch, they had flowed to the north and settled in the country between the Limpopo and the Zambesi, where they soon brought the Mashona into subjection. Their leader then had been Umsiligazi, one of Chaka's generals ; their king now was Lobengula, the son of Umsiligazi.

With a climate not extreme, the country of the Matabele and Mashona, now known as Rhodesia, was large and fertile, and peculiarly suitable for pastoral purposes. The scenery was various, and not a little of it was enchanting. 'We passed through a truly lovely tract of country,' says D. C. de Waal, who travelled in those parts with Rhodes. 'The fine rivers and valleys we had to cross ; the trees and shrubs on each side, with the birds singing behind their leafy screens, and with the pheasants on the ground under them ; the exquisite beauty of the scenery around us— these, combined with the glorious weather we were enjoying that morning, rendered the country a paradise.' Rhodes himself said, thinking presumably of his childhood : 'To be in this country is surely a happier thing than the deadly monotony of an English country town.'

Since the Zulu power had been crushed, the

Matabele were the most powerful native race remaining in South Africa. They were of the same stock and had the same warlike qualities, and since their national organisation was militaristic, those qualities remained active. Looking back on the Great War, one cannot say that the Matabele were more bloodthirsty than other races, especially in view of their subsequent docility. They lived largely upon beef and sour milk, a diet that made them exceedingly vigorous. Also, their customs were peculiar, and resulted in the existence of large numbers of young men bursting with health and (one might say) fascism. These warriors, marshalled in regiments nearly a thousand strong, decorated themselves with barbaric trappings which were a suitable expression of their bodily splendour. They wore black ostrich plumes or balls of feathers on their heads, capes of ostrich feathers on their shoulders, bands of otter skin on their foreheads, and codpieces of wild-cat skin. They carried shields of speckled ox-hide and short stabbing spears, and their gleaming limbs were free to run and to kill. Full of military ardour, they were not particularly easy to control, although their king, Lobengula, was a person of no small authority and a real grandee.

VI

ALL accounts of Lobengula agree as to his
dignified appearance, in spite of his embon-
point. Over six feet high and very heavily
built, he resembled—even in a pair of socks,
a monkey-skin loincloth and a wide-awake
hat trimmed with an ostrich feather—he yet
resembled a ' majestic statue.' He was a man
who enjoyed a drink and had sixty-eight
wives ; he had a remarkable memory ; cruelty
and geniality were mingled in his nature, and
something most aristocratically hospitable and
easy-going about him led rapidly to his un-
doing. Sir Sidney Shippard (although this
gentleman was known to the Bechuana as
Marana-maka, the Father of Lies, we may
trust his account of Lobengula) found that
the king was a fine bronze in colour, was
scrupulously clean, and had a most majestic
carriage. ' He walks quite erect, with his
head thrown somewhat back and his broad
chest expanded, and as he marches along at
a slow pace with his long staff in his right

hand, while all the men around shout his praises, he looks his part to perfection.' Fat Lobengula undoubtedly was, but he was every ounce a king. Together with Kruger and Olive Schreiner, he was one of Rhodes's few really distinguished contemporaries in South Africa.

This was the monarch whose territory Rhodes wished to annex at the earliest opportunity, and he begged the High Commissioner to recommend the establishment of a formal protectorate. But Sir Hercules Robinson would not agree to this. He did not think that the British Government would eagerly assume so large a responsibility all at once. He saw, however, the dangers of delay, and was ready to agree with a suggestion from Rhodes that Lobengula might be induced to promise that he would part with no land and make no treaty with any other Power without the High Commissioner's sanction. A missionary, J. S. Moffat, undertook to negotiate the treaty, and, owing to his good standing with Lobengula and his tact, was successful. He ' got the king to admit that the Transvaal had no right to interfere in his country '—but omitted to add that the English had no right there either—and the king put his mark to the agreement on the 11th February 1888. It was a fatal step, for it gave England what amounted to an ' option ' over Matabeleland. And England in this case practically meant England personified by Rhodes.

It need hardly be said that when Rhodes had an option over anything it was apt to be almost as good as possession. Inspired by a vision of Britannia wearing seven-league boots and carrying a pot of red paint, he would when given an inch very quickly take a mile. He knew that neither the Cape nor the Imperial Government was ready to give him assistance at this stage, and would not do so until Cape or English financial interests were involved in the north : so, even before the Moffat treaty had been signed, he and Beit had sent an emissary to try and obtain from Lobengula a gold-mining concession. He felt not merely that trade follows the flag, but that the flag must first be made to follow trade, and that the Crown must shed its lustre on the concessionaire.

He now hurried to England to find out exactly how his rival concession-hunters stood with the banks and the Government, and then hurried back to Africa. He did not approach Lobengula in person, but sent three others—

including Rudd, his business partner—with a retinue of servants. These concession-hunters, on arriving in Matabeleland, found that many others had been before them—British missionaries and Scotch traders, Boers and Germans. 'They come in like wolves without my leave,' said Lobengula, 'and make roads into my country.' It made his young men restive, inclined to brandish their asse-gais, and difficult to restrain. Rhodes's agents, because they *were* Rhodes's agents, were not out for small favours—they wanted a mono-poly. Lobengula kept them hanging about for three months, but in the end they made him put his mark and seal to a document of which he certainly did not grasp anything like the implications. It granted the agents 'exclusive power over all metals and minerals' in his kingdom, and the authority to expel all other claimants to any of that power. In return they were to pay him £100 a month and to deliver to him a thousand rifles with ammunition. That the poor old monster, sandwiched between his impatient subjects and the importunate whites, did not know what he was doing is self-evident, and is confirmed by his letter to Queen Victoria, in which he says pathetically, 'If the Queen hears that I have given away the whole country, it is not so. I do not understand where the dispute is, because I have no knowledge of writing.'

For the actual document, once obtained, Providence arranged a hair's-breadth escape from loss or destruction. Rudd, who was carrying the paper, nearly died of thirst in the Bechuanaland desert and only just managed to hide it in an ant-bear's burrow before losing consciousness. But God was clearly helping those who helped themselves, and although Rhodes's difficulties in the north were by no means at an end, he was now ready to go to London again to obtain official recognition of his efforts. The way had been partly smoothed for him by a comment appended by the High Commissioner to a copy of the Rudd concession when forwarding it to the Colonial Office. This comment was apparently not meant ironically, and yet, if the tongue of Sir Hercules was at all mobile, it must have been in his cheek while he plied his pen. ' I trust, therefore,' he wrote, ' that the effect of this concession to a gentleman of character and financial standing will be to check the inroad of adventurers as well as to secure the cautious development of the country with a proper consideration for the feelings and prejudices of the natives.' Even in Kruger's opinion Sir Hercules was 'an honourable man and a gentleman in the best sense of the word,' so perhaps the recommendation was made in good faith.

When Rhodes reached England in March 1889 he had before him the double task of seeking precedence of other syndicates and of obtaining a charter to administer and exploit the interior of Africa. He managed the first part of it by incorporation ; and the second, in the face of considerable opposition, by cultivating useful people and obtaining the support of potential enemies. He won over W. T. Stead, at that time a powerful journalist, and others, and he won over Parnell and the Irish party, who could have done him harm, by a handsome contribution to the party funds. The application for the charter specified the following objects :

(1) To extend the railway and telegraph northwards towards the Zambesi.

(2) To encourage emigration and colonisation.

(3) To promote trade and commerce.

(4) To develop mincrals and other concessions under one powerful organisation, so as to avoid conflicts between competing interests.

The charter was granted, mainly because Lord Salisbury and others felt that, although Rhodes's objects would be more properly accomplished by the Government, the House of Commons would certainly not vote the money for the purpose, and action of some sort seemed necessary. The power granted by the charter bordered on the fantastic. With no limit to the north, the Chartered Company was practically given a free hand. Its capital was fixed at £1,000,000, and, as may be imagined, the promoters did not overlook their own interests —they received 90,000 shares and a half-share in any future profits, while Rhodes brought out 125,000 shares to dispose of in Africa, and we may be sure that those into whose possession they passed were ready to give him political support if only for their pockets' sake. The English public, we are told, ' were fascinated by the promise of wealth in the new country,' and the Dukes of Fife and Abercorn joined the Board of the Company. The territory in question soon came to be known as Rhodesia, which naturally gratified Rhodes. ' Has anyone else had a country called after their name ? ' he said later, when the name was officially recognised. ' Now I don't care a damn what they do with me ! ' Other suggestions for the name of the new country had been 'Rhodesland,' and, apparently quite seriously, ' Cecilia.'

A deputation was sent to Lobengula to announce, on behalf of Queen Victoria, the granting of the charter and to advise him to give the Company his support. It included a corporal and a trooper of the Blues in full-dress uniform. The old king tapped their cuirasses and asked if they were afraid to fight without having their bodies protected. He evidently had not the faintest conception of the significance of the announcement.

VII

LOBENGULA, who is said to have had 'an extraordinary dislike to come to a definite decision upon any subject, coupled with an extreme unwillingness to say No,' was now faced, not with the arrival of a few white men to dig holes in the ground for 'shining dirt,' but with the prospect of a systematic invasion of his country. ' Did you ever see a chameleon catch a fly ? ' he had once asked a missionary. ' The chameleon gets behind the fly and remains motionless for some time, then he advances very slowly and gently, first putting forward one leg and then another. At last, when well within reach, he darts out his tongue and the fly disappears. England is the chameleon and I am that fly.' Hearing of the proposed pioneer expedition he refused to admit it, and Dr. Jameson, who had previously visited him in the course of a hunting trip and cured him of an attack of gout, was sent to try and talk him over.

Rhodes was once asked why, amongst those

who were helping him to carry out his intentions, there were several doctors. ' I like doctors for my work,' he replied, ' because, when there is blood-letting to be done, they are less squeamish.' If this was a joke (as has been claimed), it was not a very funny one. Of Rhodes's blood-letters Jameson was, of course, the most remarkable. Of the same age as Rhodes, this young Scotchman, the son of a somewhat temperamental Writer to the Signet, had been obliged, after brilliant beginnings in his profession, to come out to Africa for the cure of a weak lung. He had attended Pickering and had succeeded him as Rhodes's house-mate in Kimberley, where he established an excellent practice, which he only gave up under the double stress of Rhodes's influence and his own as yet unsatisfied love of adventure and glory. A small, bright man, he had a character of a certain complexity. He is described as volatile, mercurial, devil-may-care—' Rub it with a brick,' he once told a fanciful patient who complained of a pain in her back—and there was a charm, a kindly irony in his manner, which earned him the nickname ' Doctor Jim,' and made people like and willingly serve him. It is important to note the contrast between Jameson and his leader. While Rhodes plodded steadily along his own line of thought, and with the childlike perception of genius continually found novelty in the obvious, Jameson was sympathetic and quick to adapt himself to the point of view of others—in his quickness and impulsiveness there was indeed something rather rare in men, something feminine. The two natures were complementary, each supplying what the other lacked ; they were in a sense, to use a vulgarism, soul-mates ; and mutual affection helped to hold them together.

The influence which Jameson obtained over his fellow-men can perhaps be to some extent explained in terms of his profession. He approached political matters with the breeziest of bedside manners, as if all the world was his patient. He diagnosed ; he prescribed ; he conquered. His diagnosis was apt to err, as in clinical matters such as his failure to recognise smallpox in Kimberley ; and his cure, in the most important case of all, proved only a nostrum. But though his imagination was apt to get away with him, though something of the schoolboy and something of the actor can be discerned in his behaviour ; though, in fact, a bee or two found hiving-room in his bonnet, Jameson was no quack, but an able man. He now succeeded in getting Lobengula (whose premises were becoming rapidly clogged up with presents from white adventurers—rifles, waggons, and cases of liquor) to agree at least to the entry into his domains of Rhodes's gold-seekers.

Although this permission was soon withdrawn, the thin end of the wedge was rapidly driven home. It was decided not to provoke Lobengula unduly by going into Matabeleland itself, but by taking a route to the south of Buluwayo to make for the country of the Mashona, a gentler people, and then work northwards. The preparations were hasty, for the Dutch were also proposing a northward trek, and, said Rhodes, 'You cannot allow a single Boer to settle across the Limpopo until our position in the north is secure.' The pioneers were recruited, drilled, equipped, and combined with a force of police and a company of Bechuana natives to act as roadcutters. They left Macloutsi on the 27th June 1890, under the leadership of F. C. Selous, and the spell of that romance never absent from any of Rhodes's undertakings. What could be more romantic than the prospect they had before them of fifteen gold claims and a three-thousand-acre farm each as their share of the loot ?

These pioneers of Rhodesia, that ' heartless land,' were a mixed lot—Nimrods who derived self-satisfaction from having slaughtered some wild creature only a few hundred of whose kind existed in the world ; younger sons exiled for putting scullery-maids in the family way ; ' clean-limbed ' cricketers, butchers and bakers, Americans, Irishmen, Dutchmen, Jews. The majority, no doubt, were just enterprising and hare-brained young ' Britishers ' glad to join in an adventure which promised enrichment. ' That many poor wretches,' said General Joubert in a speech to his fellow-burghers, ' and disappointed speculators from all nations of the world, misled by fortune-hunting, are attracted to the scene of injustice and violence need not surprise you,'—but this sentence did not perhaps come best out of a Boer beard. Among the ' poor wretches ' was Major Leonard, who kept a diary in that mingled strain of facetiousness and ferocity not seldom to be found among army officers towards the end of the last century. ' As for the Matabele,' says this diarist, ' Rhodes will make short shrift of them if he gets the chance, or, if they do not give it to him, he and Jameson between them will make it, as sure as eggs are eggs ! '

The expedition was successful, and on the 11th September the place now called Salisbury was reached, and up went the usual flag. An express letter was sent to Rhodes. ' When at last I found that they were through to Fort Salisbury,' he said, ' I do not think there was a happier man in the country than myself.' Yet another ' dream ' had come true, and the activities of the Company soon spread beyond the Zambesi as far as Lake Nyassa and Lake Tanganyika. Rhodes's hopes of a rapid linking-up of the Cape with Cairo were only checked by the Anglo-German treaty which extended German East Africa to the borders of the Congo.

Meanwhile he had occupied himself anew with Cape politics. A mediocre politician, Sir Gordon Sprigg, had resigned the office of Prime Minister, and the Governor sent for Rhodes, finding that he was the only man able to carry with him enough support from both English and Dutch—Hofmeyr, the leader of the Bond party, which mainly represented the moderate Dutch farming interests, preferring to exercise his influence in opposition. Rhodes lost no time in forming his ministry—and there

he was, at the age of thirty-seven, Chairman
of De Beers and of the Gold Fields Company,
Managing Director of the Chartered Company, and Prime Minister of the Cape. But
he was much more than this. In him was
focussed the very spirit of his age, and his
deeds were an outward and visible sign of its
principal tendency—the tendency to regard
material wealth and national glory as synony-
mous ideals and to increase them by any
means and to any extent. He had shown the
world not only that he knew what he wanted
but that he was able to get it. He was everywhere recognised as a great man in mid-
career, and in the glamour of that situation
he was to remain for the next five years. In
the several spheres of his influence he was
practically a dictator.

It is impossible not to admire his energy.
In the House of Assembly he held the attention
of its occupants by his simple, direct and
almost familiar utterance, and even his opponents had to respect his common sense and
ability. Like his ancestors he thought of the
land, and created a ministry of agriculture.
He saved the oranges from disease by import-
ing an American ladybird ; he saved the wool
by his Scab Act ; he fostered the wine trade,

and improved the local breed of horses by introducing Arab stallions. He entered into questions of tariffs, railways, telegraphs, and inter-colonial co-operation, besides passing the Franchise and Ballot Act and the Glen Grey Act. He was also responsible for the annexation of Pondoland, where he had a field of maize mown down with Maxim guns by way of an object-lesson to the natives. 'And that is what will happen to you and your tribe,' he said to the chief, ' if you give us any further trouble.'

He had found time for a visit to the north. Heavy rains prevented him from visiting Mashonaland, ' his own ' country, but he had an interview in Pretoria with Kruger, the nature of which probably had a strong influence on the future dispositions of both men. Nobody was so much disliked by Rhodes as a man whom he could not persuade, and Kruger was one of those rare people who had little difficulty in withstanding his insidious persuasiveness. On this occasion Rhodes proposed nothing less than that they should work together to rob the Portuguese of Delagoa Bay.

VIII

AGAIN and again Rhodes had had reason to be apprehensive about Boer incursions into the north. Kruger always maintained that Rhodes had instigated the murder of Piet Grobler, an envoy he had sent to Lobengula, but the accusation would have been hard to prove. Apart from that, the Dutch did not remain altogether unaware of the opportunities that awaited the white man in the interior, and in March 1891 advertisements appeared in the Transvaal papers asking for volunteers to found a republic in north-east Mashonaland. Rhodes and Sir Henry Loch hurried to England, and in April the Queen issued a proclamation declaring a protectorate over Matabeleland and warning trespassers that they would be prosecuted. In June, however, a party of Boers under Colonel Ferreira actually crossed the Limpopo, but they were met by Jameson, who told them that they could only remain if they came under the authority of the Company, and this most of them agreed to do. Once he was sure of his ground Rhodes did not discourage Dutch settlers : to welcome them was politically expedient, and in accordance with his policy, so long as they stayed under the Union Jack.

Later in the year he travelled up from Beira to Umtali. He did his best to strengthen the morale of the settlers, who were not unnaturally enduring hardships, and found Jameson acting most successfully as administrator—so capable was the doctor that he reduced the police from 700 to 100, and the annual expenses from a quarter of a million for the first year to £40,000. By exerting all his influence Rhodes had managed to browbeat the Portuguese into abandoning claims they had made to certain of the northern territories, and now there remained, so far as Rhodesia was concerned, only one great obstacle in his way—the presence, or rather the independence, of the Matabele. An excuse for getting rid of this obstacle was found in the behaviour of the Matabele themselves, who had taken to raiding the neighbouring Mashona tribes. They declared that the Mashona had been stealing their cattle, and by way of revenge they murdered, robbed or drove into captivity not a few of the offenders. Although they did not attack any white men, they did not hesitate to attack white men's servants and seriously disorganised the labour supply in Mashonaland. Jameson accordingly sent a message to Rhodes saying that he proposed to fight the Matabele, and began to make preparations for war.

It was said in Africa that Rhodes had begun the trouble by telling Lobengula that the Mashona had been stealing cattle and should be punished, and that he then demanded the punishment of Lobengula for massacring the Mashona. Although the role of agent-provocateur does not seem inconsistent with Rhodes's unscrupulousness, the story seems far-fetched, and is, so far as I know, unsupported by evidence. Whether it is true or not, Rhodes, in Kruger's words, 'had his way and his war.' He and Jameson had obviously long been of opinion that the development and administration of the country could only be accomplished by a process that had been gracefully described as ' crushing and welding the Matabele into shape,' and in addition the settlers had not found Mashonaland quite ' the expected Eldorado either for mining or farming ' —in fact, they were casting greedy eyes on the fertile uplands and fat pastures of the Matabele, and resented the independence of that

tribe. 'As soon as they [the Matabele] interfere with our rights I shall end their game,'
Rhodes had said to a Dutchman as early as
1890 ; ' I shall then ask for your aid and be
very glad to get it, and when all is over I shall
grant farms to those who assisted me.'

The preliminaries of the war were as unpleasant as might be supposed. Early in 1892
Jameson had several natives shot merely on
suspicion of their having been involved in the
death of a white adventurer, and was reproved
by the Colonial Office for referring to them as
' rebels.' A Captain Lendy shot a chief and
a score of his people for ' impertinence,' but
was not removed from his authority. As for
the trouble with the Mashona, ' It is bad,'
Lobengula told the High Commissioner, ' if
you mix yourself up with such matters. Why
don't you leave the natives to settle their own
disputes ? ' As late as August 1893, Loch
wrote that Lobengula was anxious for peace,
trying to restrain his people, and to protect
the lives of Europeans in Buluwayo. In the
other camp, the white settlers who enrolled
themselves in the Company's forces had no
intention of wasting their time in a mere
punitive expedition. Their motive was robbery by force. They meant to take no mere

soldiers' pay for their efforts, but insisted on plunder—the right to mark off, after the campaign, a farm of six thousand acres and twenty gold claims, and a share of any cattle taken.

On the 5th October 1893, a patrol of the Bechuanaland Border Police were fired on near Macloutsi by some stray Matabele, and this incident was the Serajevo of a ten weeks' war. The campaign, after Rhodes had anxiously telegraphed a biblical quotation to Jameson, was virtually a walk-over for the whites, equipped as they were with ' a good supply of maxims and field-guns,' and Lobengula took refuge in retreat, after blowing up his royal kraal. The whites entered Buluwayo on the 4th November. On the 10th December Lord Ripon telegraphs to the High Commissioner, saying he has heard that ' Dr. Jameson is marking out townships in Matabeleland . . . patrols are continuing to seize large numbers of cattle from the Matabele ; the followers of Lobengula are dying of smallpox and starvation ; and the Matabele are being prevented from sowing until they surrender their arms.' Soon after the New Year the chiefs submitted, and on the 23rd January Lobengula, with whom were several of his sick and hungry regiments, died of smallpox

on the banks of the Shangani river. The war
had confirmed the British in their possession
of nearly half a million square miles of land,
and by the end of January over nine hundred
new farm rights had been issued and nearly
ten thousand gold claims registered.

We are familiar to-day with the anti-pacific
tendencies of members of Parliament and
others who hold shares in armament firms,
and it would be interesting to know exactly
to what extent the feeble behaviour of the
Imperial Government in regard to Matabeleland was conditioned by weakness or indifference, and to what extent by financial interests
in the Chartered Company. This so-called
' First Matabele War ' was promoted mainly
by Rhodes and Jameson ; the Company bore
the whole expense of the campaign ; and
when it was over the Imperial authorities
allowed Rhodes to go on having his own way.
In the following year, ' in recognition of his
great work,' he was made a Privy Councillor.
' I made the seizure of the interior a paramount
thing in my politics,' he said in a speech, ' and
made everything else subordinate.' He had
now seized the interior, and the main part of
his life's work was done.

Olive Schreiner once made an analysis of

English motives and methods in colonisation. She pointed out that the Frenchman, in taking another people's country, believes and declares it to be for the honour and glory of his own. The Boer, wishing to annex a native territory, says : ' The damned Kaffir ! I'll take his land from him and divide it among my children.' But the Englishman, having allowed a handful of adventurers to penetrate a new country, declares that they must be protected, decides that the natives are benighted and must be reformed (' It's a very sad thing the way these natives go on ! It's my duty to interfere . . .), murmurs a few phrases about ' right being on our side,' obtains meanwhile most valuable concessions, quotes from the Bible, opens fire with machine-guns, and is soon in possession, with his ubiquitous flag breezily proclaiming the fact overhead. The Englishman, in fact, deceives himself, and deserves to be called a hypocrite. He does not say, ' I hate,' ' I love,' 'I want,' but 'I think I ought—,' 'It is my duty to—,' 'It is only right that I should—,' or 'I'll teach them a lesson.' Rhodes himself once spoke of this ' unctuous rectitude ' of his countrymen, which he discerned in the attitude of some of them towards himself.

It would have been at least straightforward

to have shot or deported Lobengula outright,
to have grabbed his country and enslaved his
people, instead of getting him to sign papers
he did not properly understand, giving him
presents of champagne which aggravated his
gout, and then, as in the case of Jameson,
earning his gratitude by alleviating that com-
plaint. A deliberate annexation or conquest
of what is now Rhodesia would have had strong
arguments in its favour, but the British invasion of those parts was marked by humbug
and dishonesty. Lip-service was paid in
London to philanthropic principles, and the
crackle of rifle-fire soon broke out, like a
cynical echo, in Africa. We too have our
witch-doctors, and the flutter of a surplice
can always be caught sight of between the
machine-guns. In deference, perhaps, to the
nominal principles of our State religion and
to the agitation of some of the more humane
and thoughtful of our countrymen at that
time, the charter granted in the name of
Queen Victoria to the British South Africa
Company had stipulated that ' careful regard
shall always be had to the customs and laws
of the class or tribe or nation, especially with
respect to the holding, possession, transfer, and
disposition of lands and succession thereto.'

Sir Henry Loch had, in the Queen's name, repeatedly assured Lobengula that there was no design on his land ; the Company had told the same story to the British Government; but Dr. Jameson, backed and inspired by Rhodes, did not hesitate to arrange with his pack of freebooters to ' smash the Matabele ' in consideration of receiving each a liberal share of the loot. ' There was nothing,' says Lord Olivier, ' that was admirable in the Matabele dominion, the last of the bloody tyrannies begotten by Chaka. There was nothing that was not discreditable in the fraud, provocation and slaughter by which its destruction was engineered. Throughout the last acts of that conflict Lobengula made a far better showing for the credit of human character than did the assailants of his domain.'

IX

EVENTS were now arranging themselves in such a way as to make every day more inevitable Rhodes's coming to grips with the principal enemy of his 'dreams'—Kruger, the President of the Transvaal. The 'racehorse' and the 'ox' were not likely to become easy stable-mates, and with the passing of the years Kruger came to regard the English policy in South Africa as 'lies, treachery, intrigues, and secret investigation against the government,' while Rhodes became for him in due course someone scarcely to be mentioned by name and referred to (so it is said) as 'that murderer.' It would be very convenient for the biographer if Kruger could be made to play the role of hero against Rhodes as villain, or vice versa, but we are obliged to respect both men for their vigour, determination and originality, and at the same time we remain well aware of the failings which both men made so plain. Those of us who do not waver in upholding the principles of rigid nationalism must regard them as model exponents—one of the policy of conquest by limitless expansion and absorption, the other of the equally proud policy of primitive isolation. And even the waverers and the sceptics must realise how nice it must be to feel that all one's behaviour springs from a single infallible ideal, and at the same time helps to make that ideal a reality.

Oom (' Uncle ') Paul, born so long ago as 1825, was rather a grandiose figure. As hardy as a cave-man, he had been a lion-killer at fourteen ; at running, riding and shooting he had excelled ; and the story has often been told of how he amputated his own thumb with a penknife, and fought the subsequent gangrene with turpentine. The story of his life is the story of one long attempt to escape from British interference and domination. He had left the Cape in the 'thirties with the Voortrekkers, whose intention that was. After forty years his bugbear was still hot in pursuit, and articulate in the preposterous ejaculation of Sir Garnet Wolseley in 1879, ' So long as the sun shines, the Transvaal will be British territory ; and the Vaal river shall flow back to its sources before the Transvaal is again independent.' He survived to contend with all the machinations of Rhodes and Rhodes's supporters, and in the end had to leave his country.

Like Rhodes he felt himself to be an instrument of destiny, and unlike Rhodes he was sustained throughout his life by the effort to be a Christian. If Kruger's Christianity was of the depressing Judaic God-is-on-our-side variety (' Christ is our Commander-in-Chief,' he announced during the Boer War) and kill-joy as well (' His Honour considers a ball as Baal's service '), it seems to have been sincere. A tough old man, he resembled Rhodes in that he knew his own mind but not its limitations. But where Rhodes had vast aims and the backing of an Imperial power at its zenith, Kruger only wanted independence for his little republic of rough-and-ready farmers—like the Matabele, they had only won their country and their freedom after years of hardship and fighting, and they not unnaturally wished to keep what they had obtained with such difficulty. Kruger had the downrightness of a peasant and something of the impressiveness of a patriarch, but for all his shrewdness was no diplomat. He was a die-hard, and a stranger to the useful art of compromise. Like other notable instruments of destiny (Gandhi is an example), he was an obstacle in the way of what the world considers to be progress. At once the Moses, the Lansbury, and the Grand Old Woman of the Transvaal, he was most particularly an obstacle in the way of what Rhodes considered to be progress.

As the time for the duel between the two men drew near, a certain change came over Rhodes. His natural arrogance and impatience became intensified. For years he had 'done much for the Imperial power without official sanction, sometimes in the face of official discouragements, but always with popular approval and official recognition in the end,' and this had led him to think ' that he held a sort of general power of attorney from his Queen and country to do virtually what he wanted in South Africa.' In short, power had turned his head. Used to having his own way, urged on by flatterers, and haunted, owing to his heart trouble, by the thought that he had very little time left in which to do what he wanted, the plethoric magnate was now getting ready to take the step which proved to be his greatest blunder.

With the idea of South African federation never long out of his mind, and with a clear understanding that it would be impossible without Dutch co-operation, Rhodes had persistently tried to get Kruger to agree to a federal system which should leave the Transvaal and Orange Free State republics independent, while establishing at least a customs union, equal railway rates, and a common court of appeal between all the states concerned. But Kruger no doubt felt that such a system would be far too like making common cause with Rhodes, the exemplar of his dearest antipathies, and he clung with the utmost doggedness to his prejudices and principles. So there had gradually come into being an important conflict between those who cherished the ideal of a united British South Africa, inspired by Rhodes and affording room and representation under equal institutions for Dutchmen, and those who shared Kruger's hope that one region of South Africa at least should preserve its own Dutch character and owe no allegiance to the Crown. The scene of that conflict was the Witwatersrand.

The discovery of gold at Johannesburg in the middle 'eighties had, of course, led to a gold rush on a large scale. The great influx of immigrants and the richness of the reef, which was rapidly developed, had caused a large town to come into being. The immigrants were known as Uitlanders, this term being used to denote any settler in the Transvaal not Dutch by birth and not naturalised, and it was especially applied to British settlers. Numerous and active, the Uitlanders had turned a poverty-stricken backveld state into a country with an important income. The figures speak for themselves. In the ten years after the discovery of gold, the total revenue of the Transvaal rose from £178,000 to £3,000,000.

Dr. Leyds, a Hollander, who was one of Kruger's right-hand men, had once described his master as ' an ignorant, narrow-minded, pig-headed, and irascible old Boer,' and it must be said that Kruger's policy in regard to the Uitlanders might justly be considered a triumph of stupidity. Instead of trying to turn them into contented citizens, he denied them all political and municipal rights, and treated them not simply as outsiders but almost as enemies. He considered that the goose that laid the golden eggs ought never to be allowed to cackle. His view was that these people who had thrust themselves upon his country were mostly of the scum of the earth ; that they had shown no signs of loyalty towards the Transvaal ; and that, although they had enriched his treasury, they had enriched themselves much more. So why, he argued, should they clamour for representation? As far back as 1886 he had been advised by President Brand of the Orange Free State to make friends with the miners by offering them every possible concession. But he remained obstinate, and clung fast to the opinion that small concessions would lead to great ones.

The grievances of the Uitlanders accumulated until they were past counting. They rightly complained that the Government was not only repressive but dishonest, corrupt, inefficient and ridiculous. It was dishonest because on the 8th August 1881, on taking over the administration of the country, the Pretoria Government had expressly declared, ' To all inhabitants, without exception, we promise the protection of the law, and all the privileges attendant thereon.' It was inefficient if only because it was wasteful. Bribery and nepotism were rampant, the influence of Hollander and of German concessionaires had been proved and was resented, and there were grounds for fearing German intervention in Transvaal politics. The destruction of locusts had been opposed in the Volksraad (parliament) because they were to be regarded as a plague sent by God as punishment for sins; opposition had arisen to the erection of pillar-boxes on the ground that they were effeminate; and a motion for the abolition of barmaids had been seriously discussed.[1] The Uitlanders had no vote and no local government; Dutch was the language of instruction in the schools; monopolies and concessions for coal, for dynamite, for railways, added much to the expense of mining and the cost of living; the taxpayers' money was wasted; there was interference with the High Court, and the maladministration of justice by minor officials caused much unrest; the right to trial by a properly constituted jury was denied; native affairs were mismanaged; the supply of native labour was expensive and ill-regulated or not regulated at all, and it was complained that the natives were being allowed too much liquor—for from a mine-owner's point of view it is naturally more profitable to lose one's employees from miner's phthisis than from drink.

To remedy their position the Uitlanders formed a committee which made strong repre-

[1] Tradition is powerful in South Africa, for this enlightened measure has been recently passed by the Union Government.

sentations in various quarters, and a petition bearing many thousands of signatures was presented at Pretoria, where it was treated with contempt. Indeed, contempt was the keynote of all Kruger's dealings with the Uitlanders, and it became clear to all parties concerned that there would soon be serious trouble. As if Kruger had not been unpleasant enough, he was urged by some of his own people to suppress firmly the rebellious tendencies of Johannesburg, but he replied that ' you must give the tortoise time to put out its head before you can catch hold of it.'

Since it was plain that there would sooner or later be a rising, Rhodes determined to organise it. By forcing the issue of the Johannesburg trouble he would obviously force the issue between himself and Kruger, so that the Imperial Government would have to intervene and make a settlement. Beit was to share the expenses ; Jameson was to be put in command of a force on the Bechuanaland border, where Rhodes had obtained a strip of land ostensibly for railway construction, as well as the right to maintain an armed force at Pitsani, ostensibly to protect the construction parties. Rhodes explained his motives. He said he wished to get rid of abuses which affected him as an important mine-owner, and he wanted to force Kruger to agree to free trade between the various South African states, because 'from that will flow a customs union, railway amalgamation and ultimately federation.'

X

ACTIVE preparations were made both in Johannesburg and on the border, where Jameson now commanded a force of some six hundred, composed mostly of men of the Mashonaland Mounted Police and the Bechuanaland Border Police, and led mostly by young Guards officers who had been seconded for police work, had little military experience, and displayed ' the light-hearted carelessness of cheery schoolboys.' If there was a touch of youthful ebullience at Pitsani, there was a touch of melodrama in the behaviour of the ringleaders. Mysterious telegrams were exchanged, in which the plot was referred to as the ' flotation ' or the ' polo tournament,' and some of them are slightly reminiscent of *Alice in Wonderland* : ' Have seen Saufinder,' wired Beit to Phillips, ' mitzdruse to schaffiger bleimass absolutely that Chairman hablohner on flotation no request or letter is hobelspane as anlegspan is ausgerodet as previously angelstern.' The stage-whisper in which the conspirators discussed their secret was quickly carried and distorted by rumour, and in Pretoria as well as Cape Town it was known that there was something afoot. Arms and ammunition were smuggled into the Transvaal in oil-drums or under loads of coal, and an active part was played by officials of De Beers at Kimberley and of the Chartered Company at the Cape. Rhodes himself was able to use the advantages of his position as Prime Minister to try and further his interests as gold-magnate.

It was one of his principles to give a free hand to his subordinates if he thought they knew what he was after—an excellent principle, and one which encouraged both responsibility and initiative. Provided that they were successful, he did not quibble over the ways by which success had been obtained. In the case of Jameson, however, his usual plan did not work, for he put too much faith in the doctor's brilliance and overestimated his level-headedness. That he made such a mistake after knowing Jameson for twenty years is one of various indications that he knew more about big business than human nature.

Jameson managed to obtain from the Johannesburg leaders a letter of invitation to himself, calling for his aid on the strength of a trumped-up account of how the Transvaal Government had 'called into existence all the elements necessary for armed conflict,' and of how, in the event of that conflict, ' thousands of unarmed men, women and children of our race ' would be ' at the mercy of well-armed Boers, etc.' The date of this letter was purposely left blank, so that he could fill it in when he started and use the letter to try and justify his invasion of Dutch territory.

By no means all of the ' reformers ' in Johannesburg were hot for revolt. They were divided ; some did not know what they wanted, and many did not greatly care what they got ; and there were endless arguments as to whether they were to shed their blood for the Union Jack or just to try and get a vote under the Vierkleur. It was clear to Rhodes that until they were readier and more united any direct action must be postponed. ' I can keep Jameson on the frontier six months or nine months,' he said, ' it matters not how long—till your plans and your armament are complete, and your action will have a reasonable chance of success.' But Jameson, whose destiny and character had fitted him to conduct the most theatrical exploit in South

African history, grew tired of delay, and decided that if he was going to do anything he must play the strong man and that at once. If the Uitlanders would not rise, well, they should be jockeyed into rising. ' You may say what you like,' he is reported to have said, ' but Clive would have done it ! '

On Sunday morning, the 29th December 1895, Rhodes received a telegram from Jameson saying that he was starting for Johannesburg that night. He drafted a reply, ordering him not to move, but the telegraph offices were shut for the day—though it might be supposed that a Prime Minister would have had influence enough to open them, had he wished to do so —and by the evening the wires had been cut by Jameson. At Pitsani the day had been spent in a vocal and alcoholic celebration of the easy success anticipated by the filibusters. A trooper sent to cut the wires to Pretoria was so drunk that he ' carefully cut and buried long strands from a farmer's fence ' by mistake, so that Kruger was kept well informed of the progress of the troops. The principal motive force of those troops was Rhodes's ' dream,' and the secondary one was Jameson's vanity. If that quixotic physician had ' stuck to Epsom salts,' it would have been more to his credit, for now, so absorbed was he in the vision of himself as a Clive, or Garibaldi, or knight-errant, that he did not hesitate to act as though he was a qualified soldier and to gamble with the lives of men he was unfit to command. As if it was not enough to carry out an act of war without authority, he was not even business-like ; the arrangements for the march were wretched, and the men were tired and hungry before they walked straight into the encircling Boer commandos at Doornkop and were obliged, not without losses, to surrender. A final touch of bathos was not wanting. The white flag raised on this historic occasion was not, as has been said, a shirt torn from the back of a hero, but an apron borrowed from an old Hottentot *tanta*, or mammy, who happened to be at hand, wondering, no doubt, what all the fuss was about.

The repercussions were widespread and immediate. Rhodes had a heart-attack, and resigned his premiership ; Sir Hercules Robinson left for Pretoria, where Jameson and his officers had been imprisoned ; Grey succeeded Jameson as Administrator of Rhodesia ; and the Kaiser sent his famous telegram to Kruger : ' I tender you my sincere congratulations that,

without appealing to the help of friendly
Powers, you and your people have been successful in opposing with your own force the
armed bands that have broken into your
country to disturb the peace ; in restoring
order and in maintaining the independence of
your country against attacks from without.'
This had something of the effect upon England
that outside interference has upon a man who
is beating his wife. The British Fleet was
ordered out, and the supposed German menace
diverted attention to some extent from the
Raid.

There is a common idea that Rhodes behaved very finely by refusing to dissociate
himself from Jameson and Jameson's action.
His loyalty to his friends is not in question.
He could not in this matter so dissociate himself, for the simple reason that he was impli-
cated in it, and the evidence to prove that fact
was bound to be made public. ' I have been
so intimately connected with Jameson,' he himself said, ' people will not relieve me of responsibility.' So when Hofmeyr told him that resigna-
tion of the premiership was not enough, and
that he must issue a manifesto repudiating
Jameson, suspending him as Administrator of
Rhodesia, and declaring that he should be

punished, Rhodes's share in the conspiracy, quite apart from his affection for Jameson, compelled him to refuse. The refusal lost him the fifteen-year-old friendship of Hofmeyr (who said he felt as if he had been ' deceived by the wife of his bosom '), as well as that of others, both Dutch and English, who considered him guilty of deceit and treachery.

Many stood by him, and some attempted to justify him. His banker, Sir Lewis Michell, saw fit to describe the Raid as a ' picturesque and irregular episode in the long duel between Republican aspirations and the settled convictions of those who preferred British institutions under the supremacy of the Crown.' Why it should be considered ' picturesque ' to try and thrust one's settled convictions upon other people who do not want them would be hard to explain. However real the grievances of the Uitlanders, the Raid itself was a fiasco —questionable as to the motive and school-boyish in the execution. The most ingenious excuse made for Rhodes was that of Sprigg. ' He was not himself,' declared that ex-premier. ' Whatever part he took in the thing was simply due to the influenza.'

There is no mystery about Rhodes's responsibility. The Cape Committee of Enquiry found that Rhodes and Beit, equally with Dr. Jameson and Dr. Harris, secretary in South Africa of the Chartered Company, were 'active as promoters and moving spirits throughout.' One who knew Rhodes has said that he was 'the *fons et origo* of the conspiracy of 1895, and he it was who engineered and made inevitable the collision that occurred in 1899.' The net result of his folly was that he lost his leadership and destroyed in a moment public and private sympathies that he had laboured for years to develop. His dictatorship was gone for ever ; his alliance with the Bond party too, for he had driven them to side with Kruger ; he had hopelessly undermined his hopes of federation ; he had lowered himself in the estimation of many thoughtful people, and in a less chauvinistic period would have ruined his credit with the Imperial Government, which deprived him neither of his privy-councillorship nor of his charter. I do not feel qualified to discuss the question of Chamberlain's awareness of Rhodes's intentions, nor do I know the exact part played by Fairfield of the Colonial Office, who was closely in touch with him as well as with Dr. Harris. National vanity ran high in England in those days, and although

Rhodes was formally censured by the Select Committee at Westminster, he was supported in the House of Commons by Chamberlain, while opinion about the Raid itself was mostly tolerant where it was not enthusiastic. As Rhodes archly explained to the Kaiser three years later, ' I was a naughty boy . . . and I never got whipped at all.' It is a little saddening to think that vast power over mankind was wielded by a man who could describe himself in such terms.

'For the time being,' he announced, after having so thoroughly queered his own pitch in the south, ' my chief work shall be the opening up of the north.' There was scarcely any other course open to him.

XI

FOR several years now the Chartered Company had persisted in its attempt to administer the vast new territories in the north. In their first report the directors had estimated the land they had usurped at 80,000,000 acres, so their hands were not exactly empty. They had appointed magistrates and other officials. Having found less gold than the shareholders had hoped for, they had seized all the cattle they could get hold of, and had branded them with the mark C.C., presumably on the principle that possession is nine points of the law. In this connection it is important to understand that for the natives their herds were not merely a source of pride but their principal wealth, by custom and usage in a sense their bank, their credit and means of exchange, from which besides they obtained food and other necessaries of everyday life ; in fact, to no small extent was their life centred in their cattle, with which was associated a wealth of traditional lore. Besides stealing cattle, the

Company had imposed forced labour, which the natives had every reason to resent—because it was forced, and because it was labour, for they were used to seeing manual labour done by their womenfolk ; because, even when willing to do ordinary farm work, they were afraid to work underground in mines (and who shall blame them ?) ; because they did not enjoy being kicked and flogged ; and because those who managed to escape were hunted down as deserters and brought back. Finally, the Company had seen fit to establish a corps of native police, considered to be of a lower caste than those whom they were set to control. These police were not properly supervised, and, following the common tendency of human beings to be hard on their own kind, abused their authority, gloried in petty tyrannies, and extorted money and women.

In view of these activities, the Matabele naturally did not regard the coming of the white men as an unmixed blessing, and it would not have been surprising if they had very soon tried again to resist it. On the contrary, we find in the report of the Company for 1894-5 that the Matabele have proved ‘ docile,’ that there has been little serious crime, and that beyond petty thefts there has not been much to complain of in their general behaviour. There are limits, strange as it may seem, to what even African natives can stand, and when it began to appear to the Matabele that Nature herself was in alliance with the white men against them, their sufferings could scarcely be borne. There had been a severe drought ; the locusts had increased ; and rinderpest, the most dreaded of cattle diseases, had broken out, with the result that such cattle as remained to them were shot down wholesale to prevent the spread of infection. A party of native women, who had refused to say where some cattle had been hidden, were shot in cold blood. On the 28th February 1896 there was an eclipse of the moon, which seemed like a sign from heaven, and at last the natives, who had, of course, heard of the capture of Jameson and his force by the Boers, could put up with their troubles no longer ; they rose up and massacred some whites on outlying farms—and they had this in common with their enemies, that they were not very nice in their methods. On the 25th March a Mr. Duncan, ' Controller of Cattle ' in Buluwayo, called a ' council of war,' and parties were sent out to ' shoot down natives indiscriminately.' On the 6th April the *Matabele Times* remarked that ' we have been doing it up to now—burning kraals because they were native kraals, and firing upon fleeing natives simply because they were black.'

When the trouble began—it is known as the ' Rebellion '—Rhodes was on his way back, via the East Coast, from a flying visit to England, where he had learnt that the charter was in no danger of cancellation as a result of his share in the responsibility for the Raid. He landed at Beira, and on hearing the news from Matabeleland hastened to Salisbury, where, though ill with malaria, he lent a hand in organising a column, with which he took part in operations against the natives. In a letter dated the 25th May we find him instructing a Major Laing to ' do the most harm you can to the natives around you,' and displaying his usual grasp of detail and gift for organisation. By the beginning of June, when he arrived at Buluwayo, an English general, Sir Frederick Carrington, had been sent out by the Imperial Government to take command. This officer, who divided the white troops into three columns, had with him two soldiers *en route* for the peerage, Colonel Plumer and Colonel Baden-Powell. It is worth noting, as an instance of the force of Rhodes's example, the dying words of Hubert Hervey, a friend of his, who was a trooper in Plumer's column. This young man, when mortally wounded and being carried in on a stretcher, was heard to exclaim : ' Who knows but that I may soon be pegging out claims for England in Jupiter ! '

There are several anecdotes belonging to this time which throw light on Rhodes. They were told by Lord Grey, who succeeded Jameson as Administrator. On one occasion Grey was fast asleep in his tent after a hard day's riding when he was suddenly woken up by Rhodes, who was standing over him in nothing but a shirt. ' What's the matter ? ' he said. ' Is the tent on fire ? ' ' No, no,' said Rhodes, ' I just wanted to ask you, have you ever thought how lucky you are to have been born an Englishman when there are so many millions who were not born Englishmen ? ' There is also the story of Grey waiting for Rhodes with a telegram in his hand, and hesitating to break some bad news—Rhodes's house, Groote Schuur, had been burned to the ground with all it contained. ' Is that all ? ' said Rhodes. ' I thought you were going to say that Jameson was dead.' Is not this a clear indication, if any be needed, that Rhodes loved property less for its own sake than for the power that it brings ? Groote Schuur was a place in which to dream his dreams, to receive his friends and command his catspaws, and its destruction, unpleasant though it was, could do no damage to his ambitions. 'What with the Raid,' he said later, ' rebellion, famine, rinderpest, and now my house burnt, I feel like Job.' No doubt there were others in Africa at that time who, thanks to his activities, also felt like Job.

The Matabele had retired into the Matopo hills, where they felt better able to hold their own than in the more open country, and it was soon realised that the campaign was resolving itself into guerilla warfare. It was seen that, while the natives were bound to be beaten in the long run, that might only be accomplished at the cost of many men and much money. General Carrington even spoke of needing a force numbering five thousand, and the Chartered Company had already had to bear considerable losses and expense. Rhodes thought the matter over carefully, and then made one of those decisions characteristic of him as of other great men—a decision at once too simple and too dangerous to have been arrived at by anybody else. His idea was to go unarmed and unguarded right among the Matopos, right among the natives, and talk things over with them. 'Surely,' he said, ' there must be reasonable men among them who will listen to me when they know that I am ready to meet them. At any rate, let us find out.' Whether there were reasonable men among the natives or not, Rhodes was ready, in the face of all objections, to trust to his personal magnetism, to his confidence in himself, to the magic armour of a charmed life, in order to get his way. He had shown himself as ready to brave the trials and dangers of the wilderness as the bulls and bears of the stock exchange; he had answered the ogreish de la Rey with a request for breakfast; he was to thread his way among the Boer bullets at Kimberley, wearing his usual white trousers and not turning a hair. Perhaps, like Frederick the Great, he believed himself bullet-proof. One thing is certain, these masters of men behave like the servants of destiny, and undertake their extraordinary tasks as a matter of course, as a matter of instinct.

Rhodes now moved to Plumer's head-quarters on the edge of the Matopos, and made his preparations. His project could hardly have been carried out without the services of a go-between, and the preliminary negotiations, which took nearly a week, were the work of one John Grootboom. A Tembu of twenty-five, this man had a knowledge of both the English and Matabele languages, and was a brave and loyal servant. He managed to get some of the chiefs to agree to a meeting, provided that Rhodes came un-armed and accompanied by only three other white men. Rhodes chose as companions his friend Dr. Sauer ; Vere Stent, a newspaper correspondent, who has written the best and I believe the only eye-witness account of the parley ; and Johan Colenbrander, a man with an unusually close experience of the natives. Everything was now ready for the enterprise.

XII

EARLY on a fine winter's morning Rhodes and his little party set out, taking Grootboom with them as guide, and riding over the rustling golden grass. At least one of them was a prey to nerves, and as they entered the hills they all realised that their retreat was cut off and that they were at the mercy of the Matabele. When they arrived at the place appointed for the parley, a little open space with a broken ant-hill in the middle, they dismounted, hitched their horses to some fallen tree-trunks, and awaited the signal of a white flag that had been agreed on. This duly appeared, and a party of natives, fully armed, were seen advancing. Twenty or thirty of them gathered round in a semicircle, and the atmosphere was so tense that it seemed as if the least indiscretion on the part of the whites might lead to a massacre. Rhodes spoke first, with a peace greeting, which was replied to. Somabulane, a chief who, like so many of his kind, was an excellent orator, then made a long speech describing some of the numerous grievances of his people. 'You may wipe out the Matabele,' he concluded, 'but you cannot make dogs of them.'

Rhodes listened attentively, and then, using Colenbrander as interpreter, followed his usual policy of taking the war into the enemy's camp. 'Why,' he asked, 'had the Matabele killed white women and children? That was not right; that was not the work of brave men; that was the work of dogs.' This was not a very good line to take, and Somabulane quickly exposed its weakness. 'Who began the killing of women?' he retorted. 'Your tax-collectors shot four women in cold blood when there was peace, because the women would not tell them where some cattle were hidden.' At this an angry murmur of assent arose from his companions. 'They're getting excited,' Colenbrander whispered to Rhodes; 'I should drop the subject.' Rhodes did as he was told, and Somabulane now returned to his grievances. He complained of a white Native Commissioner who, exercising a non-existent *droit de seigneur*, had raped a black bride on her wedding-day; of the behaviour of other white officials; of peculiarly elaborate insults to himself when he had paid a formal visit to the white officials in Buluwayo;

and of the extortions and tyrannies of the detested native police. To all this Rhodes replied in a conciliatory and reassuring way, and promised that the native police should be got rid of. Whether what he said, or the way he said it, or whether that glamour of his personality about which all men are agreed, or whether his prestige, or every one of these things, was responsible, Rhodes conquered once more. He was irresistible. He did not storm at the natives, he reassured them, he soothed them, and with a symbolical laying down of arms they surrendered. It was one of his greatest personal triumphs. Unmolested, the party rode back, Rhodes exultant, the others full of relief, and Stent commenting to himself that ' the case against the settlers and the Chartered Company's officials seemed pretty black, if one-tenth of the stories that we heard were true.'

Like most very able people, Rhodes knew how to be grateful. He was generous to all who served his aims, and often to total strangers who asked him for money. He did not forget the services of John Grootboom, and ordered that he should be given a hundred acres of land, a waggon, a span of oxen, twelve cows, a horse, and a hundred pounds, but

Grootboom, who must have been a remarkable person (for all I know, he is still living), never claimed the reward.

The matter was not yet settled. Somabulane was not the spokesman of his whole nation, and, in spite of Rhodes's show of good faith, it remained for the agreement to be ratified. Further parleying was necessary, and it had been arranged that a second *indaba* should be held a week later in a remoter place. Colonel Plumer wished to support Rhodes by keeping his troops in close attendance, but Rhodes insisted on their remaining at a distance of four miles, as he wished to gain the confidence of the chiefs. This second meeting took place on the 21st August. This time there were seven in the white party, which included Colenbrander again, his wife and sister, who were determined to go with him, and Grimmer. When they approached the chosen spot only a score of natives were visible, but as they were about to dismount they were surrounded by some five hundred warriors, threatening in appearance and fully armed with assegais and rifles. ' Stick to the horses ! ' shouted Colenbrander. ' There is treachery about ! ' But Rhodes took not the slightest notice of him, and with fine courage rode right in amongst the

natives. 'What is this?' he cried. 'How am I
to trust you? You asked me to meet you with
my friends and wished us to come unarmed,
saying you would do the same, and what do I
find? Five hundred and more fully armed
warriors. Until you lay your guns and assegais
down, and I order you to do so, all of you, I
decline to discuss any matter with you at all.'
And turning to some of the older chiefs, he
added, ' Tell these men to lay down their arms
at once, or we shall go back and the war will
go on.' Whereupon he walked up to a rock
in the midst of them and sat down on it,
leaving his followers amazed at the authority
in his bearing.

With Colenbrander again acting as interpreter, a long conversation ensued, in the course
of which old and well-founded suspicions
cropped up. 'How do we know that Rhodes
is doing his best for us?' said one native.
' Perhaps when he goes away he tells his people
to rob us.' But Rhodes, persuasive as ever,
managed to talk them round, and with their
keen sense of justice and usual ready response
to even a show of kindness the natives warmed
to him and believed him when he said, ' You
are my children, I will protect you always,
etc., etc.,' and when he and his party returned

to their camp a great part of the warriors went with them, shouting and singing. After this, Rhodes spent nearly two months holding frequent parleys with the natives, and eventually confirming the peace by ordering at the Company's expense a million bags of maize, for the Matabele had been unable to sow their lands, and if they were to starve there would clearly be no labour with which to develop the country.

In spite of Rhodes's achievements, however, the settlement was not so final as may appear. In the first place, some of Plumer's troops brought about a crisis, for they broke into the burial-place of Umsiligazi, the father of Lobengula, and king and founder of the Matabele nation, who had died in 1868. The Matabele were as superstitious as Christians, for they believed in the resurrection of the old man's body, and the place was sacred to them. The English soldiers had torn down walls of loose granite, dug up the ground in search of treasure, disturbed the skeleton, and entered a cave containing the king's possessions, which they had smashed up and strewn all over the place. Rhodes was as furious at this as the natives were grieved, for he feared the consequences. But with great tact he managed to propitiate them and to mend matters as best he could.

The Matabele were now more or less quietened down, but not so the Mashona, their former subjects, who had been looked on as an unwarlike race. The Mashona were not entirely easy to conquer. Unlike the Matabele, they had no corporate existence, but each little community was a law to itself; their strongholds were honeycombed with caves; and having been worked up into a frenzy of suggestibility by the prophecies of a half-legendary, cave-dwelling individual called Umlimo, they intended to continue to resist the invaders. The hold which such prophets obtain over Africans is best shown by the career of the Mahdi. They invariably assert that the white man's bullets will turn to water, and drive whole tribes into the most reckless follies.

The doings of the punitive expedition, sometimes dignified with the name 'Second Matabele War,' are described in a book by Lord Baden-Powell, of which both text and illustrations, with their peculiarly British blend of maudlin flippancy and ruthless efficiency, are invaluable to the student. He speaks of the campaign as ' nigger-fighting '—as one might say ' snipe-shooting ' or ' pig-sticking,' and the Chief Scout-to-be takes a boyish

delight in the 'splendid boom' as some
pathetic little Mashona acropolis is 'blown
to smithereens'—not, of course, before some
preliminary looting and a 'curio-hunt' have
cleared the huts. Yes, there must have been
a big bang as thirty-four cases of dynamite
turned a kopje, which men had called their
home, into a crater. . . .

It has been estimated that eight thousand
natives were killed in the suppression of the
'rebellion.' It was Rhodes who had decreed
that the Matabele must be 'thoroughly
thrashed,' at a time when order, in the opinion
of some, might have been established by
pacific methods. Rhodes and his Company
were determined ; the Imperial authorities
blew hot and cold ; and the mischief got
done. If Rhodes had not done it, certainly
the Germans or the Portuguese or the Dutch
or the Belgians would have been at least
equally violent. It is a sterile business trying
to fix blame too closely upon individuals in
such matters, for in a sense all parties concerned are responsible, and many a crime is
committed by estimable people who sincerely
believe that they are obeying their conscience
and doing their duty. Life being what it
is, we are all in the soup together, and it is

perfectly clear that not a few of the persons who exercise power, in any country or at any time, are to no small extent either foolish or cruel, or both, simply because they are human beings.

XIII

As far back as 1890, Rhodes had first come in touch with Olive Schreiner, who, with two or three exceptions, may well be regarded as his greatest South African contemporary. His personal contacts with her were few, but the two of them were in truth mighty antagonists, and time may prove the woman the victor, because unpopular ideas have a way of coming into their own in the long run. Rhodes, with all his merits, believed in the power that money brings, and in the continual increasing of that power at any cost ; Olive Schreiner believed that no advantage should ever be deliberately taken, either of an individual or a community, either of the Dutch or the natives, which should tend to weaken or destroy self-respect.

They began by a clear recognition of each other's powers. ' A work of profound genius,' said Rhodes of the *Story of an African Farm*. ' I am going to meet Cecil Rhodes,' said Olive, ' the only great man and man of genius South

Africa possesses.' She had a most acute sense of the subtleties of character, and it did not take her long to find out that 'that huge hard-headed man of the world' was 'curiously like a little child.' Hoping against hope, like the rest of humanity, that the great man was good, she began to feel 'a curious and almost painfully intense interest in the man and his career.' She began, in fact, to have doubts.

Her worst fears were confirmed when Rhodes voted for the so-called 'Strop' Bill, which was to give white people the right to flog their native servants. She saw that he was trying to 'throw the native as a sop to the Boer' because he wanted Dutch support for his own purposes. It was not long before Rhodes discovered the 'strongest antipathy' to her, though he could not lose sight of her ability, and indeed her influence, for her writings were much read in England at that time. She, on her part, seems to have had some vague idea that she could 'save' him —it is not, after all, very unusual to like people for what they might be rather than for what they are, nor to make the mistake of wanting those whom we admire to be perfect according to our own ideas.

'Why do you surround yourself with the

type of men you do ? ' she asked. ' Why do you make friends of such men ? '

' *Those* men my friends ! ' he replied. ' They are not my *friends* ! They are my tools, and when I have done with them I throw them away ! '

Meeting him on a station platform after he had voted for the ' Strop ' Bill, she refused to shake hands with him, turned on her heel, and walked away. ' The perception of what his character really was in its inmost depths,' she said, ' was one of the most terrible revelations of my life.' She felt that she could discern ' below the fascinating surface, the worms of falsehood and corruption creeping.'

Rhodes tried to make peace, and repeatedly sent her invitations, which she invariably refused. And then some enterprising Cape hostess gave a dinner-party at which both ' lions ' were present. Their behaviour was far from unleonine, for they were soon involved in a bitter argument, whereupon Olive burst into ' one of her tremendous storms ' and ' not only hammered her fists violently on her head and on the table but also banged her forehead on it with such force that the guests actually were alarmed lest she should injure herself.' She was determined, however, to make it clear that it was on questions of principle that she differed from him, and a few years later was explaining how strong was her 'personal admiration of Rhodes's genius,' and how strong her 'detestation of his methods, but mainly for the men who sucked the dust from his feet.' As time went on he was more and more fawned upon and toadied to by swarms of followers, who, as Basil Williams puts it, were 'not too nice in their methods.' Their flattery turned his head, and their presence 'insensibly tainted' him.

After the Jameson Raid Olive Schreiner could have made plenty of money (of which she was in need) by abusing Rhodes, and of course those persons who get a living by trading in the emotions of others were not slow to tempt her. But, said she, 'I attacked Rhodes frankly and fearlessly and endlessly when he was in power, and therefore I can afford to be quiet now.' Of Rhodes it has been said by one who knew him that his temperament was 'subject to the radical vice of phenomenal vindictiveness,' and we find him making remarks like, 'They will find that I can be just as nasty as they can,' of some supporters whom he had alienated. But Olive Schreiner, with the clear eye and independent judgment of genius, was not in the least interested in gloating over his discomfiture after the Raid. ' My feelings,' she said, ' are a strange mixture of intense personal sympathy with Rhodes in his downfall, and an almost awful sense of relief that the terrible power which was threatening to crush all South Africa is broken. . . . It is too terrible to think of what the results would have been if Jameson had *not* been defeated.' While she never lost sight of ' his master passions of ambition and greed, unrestrained by conscience,' she retained always a respect for his strength and a sympathy with his weakness. Indeed, she said she never felt an unkind feeling towards him.

Her conclusions about his policy are summed up in that passionate book, *Trooper Peter Halkett of Mashonaland*. To the original edition is prefixed a photograph of three naked natives hanged on a tree, the neck of one hideously dislocated, while a group of ' Britishers ' stand by—pipes in mouths, hats at jaunty angles— grinning with satisfaction at their handiwork. At the beginning of 1897, when Olive Schreiner and her husband were voyaging to England to publish this book, Rhodes was on board. In spite of the narrow limitations of life on board ship they did not speak a word to him, and the strain was scarcely eased when Cronwright (the husband) found Rhodes's bodyservant prowling about in his cabin, presumably in search of manuscripts. Rhodes used later to say that Olive Schreiner wrote *Trooper Peter Halkett* out of spite provoked by his once having told her that she had put all her thoughts and ideas into her first book, and was incapable of writing another. He thus added a foolish statement to an uncivil and untrue one. The intimate friend of Havelock Ellis, one of the most civilised men of our age, had her faults, but was incapable of spitefulness.

The relationship between Rhodes and Olive Schreiner boils itself down, like most South African matters, to a difference of opinion on the native question. These two individuals, had they been in a position to decide it, would have done so in fundamentally different ways.

XIV

FROM the age of seventeen Rhodes had been not a little in contact, either personally or politically, with African natives. The common white South African view of these people is reminiscent of some of the more fanciful branches of American thought, and of their perennial fruitage in books like *Is the Negro a Beast?* (Gospel Trumpet Pub. Co., Moundsville, Va., 1901) or *The Devil's Inkwell* (Houston, Texas, 1923), which sets out to establish on biblical evidence ' the everlasting, irrefutable and utter supremacy of the white man on the earth since the beginning of historical time.' Rhodes, however, took a somewhat different line. He declared that ' two thousand years lie between us and the natives,' and called them ' fellow tribesmen of the Druids,' but in this opinion he has neither the support of science nor of many people with a lifelong experience of native psychology.

There is no need to be sentimental about the Bantu. Like other human beings, they are only intermittently reasonable, and easily capable of many kinds of meanness and beastliness. Left to themselves, they tend, like people of other races, to be either lazy or violent, ignorant or irresponsible. They have also their merits. Even to-day they are still for the most part beautiful and dignified in appearance, and 'after a hundred years of merciless battering at the hands of the white man,' as Leonard Barnes reminds us, 'the native is still, as a racial group, the least corrupted form of humanity in Southern Africa.' Vivacious and pleasure-loving, the Bantu still respond to kindness when it is forthcoming, and are still capable of gratitude and loyalty. How, exactly, did Rhodes approach them? He said that 'the natives are in a sense citizens, but not altogether citizens—they are still children.' This *pensée* was obviously of no small political and commercial convenience. Passing over the bizarre theory that the indigenous inhabitants of a country are 'not altogether' citizens of it, let us admit, for the sake of argument, that the natives are in some ways like children. What of it? Are they in that so very different from the rest of mankind? There is plenty of evidence that Rhodes himself was in many ways like a child, and he treated the natives with that mixture of harshness and generosity which is more characteristic of the child or the tyrant than of the thoughtful, responsible adult man.

He took the fullest advantage of their racial inexperience and natural leisureliness, and when they showed any real independence of spirit, he did his best to crush it ; when they seemed docile, his policy was so to arrange matters that they would be obliged to work. ' We have taken away their power of making war,' he said, and ' at present we give them nothing to do,' therefore ' we want to get hold of these young men and make them go out to work, and the only way to do this is to compel them to pay a certain labour tax.' Besides this, his consistent policy was to forbid them liquor (and judging from the quality of the liquor they had been sold in the form of ' Cape smoke,' he probably did them a service) ; to deny them a vote ; to segregate them ; and to give them, in their own areas, some small control over their own affairs. His Glen Grey Act may be regarded as an effort to teach them the elements of local government on the European model, or as a clever device to make them feel that they had some say in their own destiny, or as a mixture of the two, according to the individual stand-point. What is clear is that Rhodes was determined that in any event their social and economic status was, as a matter of business, to be kept down to a level which should ensure servility to their white employers or exploiters.

Not long after the Raid a pseudonymous writer called ' Imperialist ' wrote a book to try and glorify Rhodes, and obtained two chapters from Dr. Jameson. The whole thing is naïvely propagandist, but Jameson's remarks on Rhodes and the natives are worth examining, because there is some truth in them. He says that Rhodes regarded the natives as children, and treated them as children, and was ' really, by nature, strangely and deeply in sympathy with them.' Furthermore, ' he likes to be with them.' Is it too much to draw again the conclusion that this sympathy was of somewhat the same nature as that which a child feels for other children ? Rhodes not only liked to be with them, but to join in their amusements, and at Kimberley, Jameson continues, ' his favourite recreation every Sunday afternoon was to go into the De Beers native compound, where he had built them a fine swimming-bath, and throw in shillings for natives to dive for.' This is among those numerous glimpses of Rhodes which give us some understanding of his charm.

' Imperialist ' assures us that Rhodes gave his employees not only swimming-baths but ' everything that can benefit them,' including ' enforced total abstinence, and a manufactory of mineral waters as a substitute.' For ' everything that can benefit them ' we may read ' everything that can keep them in a state of physical efficiency and mental backwardness to make them better wage-slaves for the white man.' Keep them on chemical lemonade, in fact, so that you may buy champagne with the money which their labour brings you. And so, when ' Imperialist ' tells us that Rhodes gave £50,000 to buy maize for the Matabele after the white invasion, we realise that it was not done from altruism, but because black labour would be needed to develop the country.

Here are three stories to illustrate Rhodes's approach to the ' native question ' as it presents itself in its early stages, when the white man thrusts himself into the black man's country. In October 1890, after a champagne supper at Macloutsi, he found, on leaving early in the morning, that his Cape-cart was not ready, and went into a ' terrible rage,' saying that all natives were alike and ought to be severely flogged, and leaving orders for the offending driver to be arrested and kept without food. In August 1896, when he was on his way to England to attend the Commission of Enquiry into the Raid, he arrived at Enkeldoorn and found that the Dutch settlers there were troubled by the presence of a native chief whose kraal was a few miles off and who ' refused to surrender.' He immediately said, ' We'll go out and attack the kraal,' and himself led the commando up a kopje at midnight. At early dawn the whites attacked the unsuspecting natives, who were shot like rats as they ran from their huts. Seventy of them were killed ; one white man was wounded. When the column returned to the foot of the kopje, an argument arose as to the number of natives killed, and in order to settle it Rhodes returned alone to count the bodies again. There is something ghoulish in the picture of this heavy, Semitic-looking man, wearing slightly soiled white flannel trousers and carrying a riding-crop, picking his way all alone among the beautiful corpses on that African hillside, while the groans of the wounded rose up in the incomparable freshness of the early morning air.

A year later he was in the same neighbourhood and had a talk with a police officer who told him of a fight that had lately taken place between his own men and some natives. On Rhodes asking how many of the natives had been killed, the officer replied, ' Very few, as the natives threw down their arms, went on their knees, and begged for mercy.' ' Well,' said Rhodes, ' you should not spare them. You should kill all you can,[1] as it serves as a lesson to them when they talk things over at their fires at night. They count up the killed, and say So-and-so is dead, and So-and-so is no longer here, and they begin to fear you.' This advice shows that Rhodes held the crude colonial belief that the welfare of a country can be permanently based on fear felt by the majority for a powerful ruling minority. It is

---

[1] ' That is the spirit to have—to keep on killing.' These words occurred in a speech made by a sergeant-major to the Inns of Court O.T.C. on the 19th July 1918. I have a copy of the speech before me as I write, and make no apology for referring to it here, because it seems to me not merely to echo but to express perfectly, some twenty years later, the logical development of Rhodes's sentiments. ' Get sympathy out of your head,' said the sergeant-major. ' We go out to kill. We don't care how, so long as they are killed, and so effectively put out of action.' He advocated the deliberate murder of wounded Germans and of German prisoners, and even described in some detail how ' delightful ' it is to ' caress ' a bayonet between one's fingers and then to stick it into a man's eye or lungs and ' to have the feeling of the warm blood trickling over your hands.'

a piece of evidence that Rhodes was more colonial than English by nature. Incidentally, ' Kill all you can ' seems an odd motto for a man who considers himself civilised.

Those who attempt to justify Rhodes's native policy are fond of saying that he declared himself in favour of securing ' Equal rights for all civilised men south of the Zambesi.' The facts are these. The actual words used by Rhodes were, ' Equal rights for every *white* man south of the Zambesi,' and thus he was correctly reported in the *Eastern Province Herald*. A copy of the newspaper was at once sent to him by an association of the coloured voters at the Cape, and he was asked whether he had in fact spoken the words as printed. This was on the eve of a General Election, and Rhodes was bound to consider the importance of the coloured vote. He therefore sent back the newspaper, on the margin of which he had written : ' My Motto is—Equal Rights for every civilised man south of the Zambesi. What is a civilised man ? A man, whether white or black, who has sufficient education to write his name, has some property, or works. In fact, is not a loafer.' This is a peculiar and characteristically narrow definition of a civilised man, and it is sad to discover that Rhodes was capable of juggling with so important a statement simply in order to catch votes.

He always had an obsession about the dangers of 'loafing,' not only where the natives were concerned. He could condemn a fellow-man in no terms so bitter as the word 'loafer.' To a friend at Oxford who proposed to try and make his living by writing he was foolish enough to say, ' It is not a man's work—mere loafing.' We are told that Rhodes liked reading Gibbon. Did it ever strike him that Gibbon is not remembered for having been a soldier, but for the product of his unmanly loafing? Rhodes once spoke of his brother Bernard as ' a charming fellow,' but ' in fact, a loafer.' And on his very death-bed he said to those around him, ' Why don't you play bridge instead of sitting about doing nothing ? '

We have all round us to-day pitiful examples of the disheartening and demoralising effects of indolence, among the rich as well as the poor, but there are a thousand beauties and advantages and opportunities in leisure and even in idleness, and the man of action is apt to fail to realise this. He is so busy, and he so enjoys being busy, that he forgets that it takes all sorts to make a world. The loafer, too, is a man, and he may be a good one. He is probably a loafer through no fault of his own. If Europeans and Americans had worked a little less at their machines in the nineteenth century and loafed a little more, it is conceivable that we might have been less easily rushed towards the War, and even that we might have been less subject to some of our present ills, such as that economic dislocation which allows over-production and deliberate waste to exist side by side with starvation.

XV

IN the years after the Raid, though Rhodes's political career was damaged beyond repair, his energies were fully engaged by activities of which the variety and purposefulness were characteristic of his greatness. He did not forsake politics. His voice was heard again in the House of Assembly, he took part in election campaigns, and made as much propaganda as he could in favour of his long-cherished idea of a federation of the South African states. When Chamberlain sent out Sir Alfred Milner as Governor in 1897, Rhodes did not over-assert himself, and the relationship between the two men became, and remained, entirely satisfactory and even cordial. As Milner is reputed to have declared that ' the power of Afrikanderdom must be broken,' this is perhaps not surprising.

At the Cape, in order to replace his house, Groote Schuur, which had been burnt down, Rhodes had a handsome new one built for him, in an adaptation of the local Dutch style, by the architect Herbert Baker. The old Netherlandish kind of interior, cool and free from fuss, had, during a couple of centuries, been gradually enriched with treasures from Batavia. Furniture of well-oiled teak, massive but not cumbrous ; good glass ; Oriental or Delft china ; patriarchal braziers and spittoons of brass and copper ; plain walls ; and a general aspect of spaciousness and solidity without ostentation—such were some of the characteristics of a style of decoration which Rhodes, with his architect's help, did something to encourage and perpetuate locally by adapting it to his own house. ' I want the big and simple,' he said, ' barbaric if you like.'

The fairly high standard of taste in the decoration of Groote Schuur was not always conspicuous in the behaviour of its occupants. In 1898, for instance, when a young reigning Sultan came to call, Rhodes did not take the trouble to receive him, but told a secretary to show the visitor what there was to be seen. The secretary much resented this, because it was the first time he ' had ever been asked to act as cicerone ' to one whom he ' looked on as a nigger.' He accordingly displayed a studied rudeness.

We do not require to be told that Rhodes

said he preferred the Roman character to the Greek, for it is made obvious by his appearance, his actions and his reading. His library at Groote Schuur contained, besides some *Private Histories of the Roman Emperors and Empresses*, a specially commissioned translation of all the authorities quoted by Gibbon in the *Decline and Fall*. This was unabridged, and Rhodes had paid thousands of pounds for it. In addition to Tacitus, for example, and Suetonius, and endless Fathers of the Church, the collection naturally included works ' of a decidedly erotic nature,' all suitably illustrated—much to the delight of some dependent, who cut the pictures out privily and carried them off. It seems a pity that Rhodes did not choose Tacitus as a bedside or camp-fire companion instead of his favourite Marcus Aurelius. He might then have chanced upon those vigorous words, *Auferre, trucidare, rapere falsis nominibus imperium, atque, ubi solitudinem faciunt, pacem appellant.*[1] But still, he would scarcely have applied them, as has justly been done, to not a few of the white man's activities in Africa. He read few works of fiction, but

[1] (*Agric.*, xxx. ' What they, by a misuse of terms, style government, is a system of pillage, murder and robbery, and their so-called peace is a desert of their own creation.')

is said to have enjoyed *Vanity Fair*, and is known to have been an admirer of a novel called *The Choir Invisible*, by James Lane Allen, an ebullient mixture of tushery and uplift, in which all the male characters are athletic and all the female winsome offshoots of the ' Anglo-Saxon ' race with its ' unimaginably splendid future.' It deals with ' iron-browed, iron-muscled, iron-hearted men ' who had not only ' cleft a road for themselves,' but had ' opened a fresh highway for the tread of the nation and found a vaster heaven for the Star of Empire '—whatever that may mean.

The grounds of Groote Schuur were naturally beautiful, but Rhodes much improved them by making paths, planting or cutting down trees, and establishing a small zoo. Like a later dictator, he kept some lions in a cage, and intended to build a ' lordly edifice ' of marble to house them in. Among them was a cub called Sullivan, which used to amuse Rhodes and Rudyard Kipling until, as Basil Williams frankly records, it ' became too stout to be a safe plaything for children.' Rhodes was the reverse of selfish where his house and estate were concerned. He gave the Cape Town public such free access to his property that they tore up the plants, picnicked on the verandah, and left litter in the glades. Their affection for Groote Schuur was clearly less romantic than the owner's. Indeed, so fulsome was his fondness for his grounds and the view from them that nobody seems able to write of it without dipping the pen, for the space of a few pages, in syrup. Why is such sickening emphasis laid upon this trait? Because it is exceptional to be fond of one's garden? No, it is because Rhodes spent not a little time in his garden living up to the nickname 'Builder of Dreams.' 'Why do I love my garden?' he said to a Mr. Menpes. 'Because I love to dream there. Why not come with me and dream also to-morrow morning?' And off they went to spend some 'happy hours' in a reverie-to-order.

Obsessed, as we know, with a need for action, he made a nice distinction between himself and 'mere dreamers,' none of whom, he declared, 'should be tolerated.' And yet he must have been aware from his own experience that the persons vulgarly considered 'dreamers' often profoundly influence mankind, and give conscious expression to the waves of sentiment which sweep it on from one crusade to another. His own Imperialist 'message' was voiced not only by himself but by Kipling. So he built a

cottage in the grounds of Groote Schuur ' for
artists and poets to stay in and draw inspiration from the Mountain '—through a tap, as
it were. Unfortunately, when turned on, the
tap seems to have produced little but mountain mist and a few hiccups of patriotic
fervour. But Rhodes himself had really no
need to draw inspiration from scenery, when
it was so easily to be found in himself. He
could always draw upon the inexhaustible
reservoir of his obsession and his sentimentality.
' When I find myself in uncongenial company,' he said, ' or when people are playing
their games, or when I am alone in a railway
carriage, I shut my eyes and think of my great
idea. I turn it over in my mind and try to
get new light on it. It is the pleasantest
companion I have.'

Let it not be thought that Rhodes spent his
last phase brooding in the garden or in railway
carriages. The Raid, fatal as it was to him,
was not exactly his Waterloo, and in these
few after-years he was extremely active. He
knew he was not going to live long, and would
often work sixteen hours a day in the service
of his ' dreams.' He bought nearly thirty
fruit-farms at the Cape, and by bringing
experts from California, and general good

management, so developed them that he may be said to have practically founded the South African fruit export trade. At Inyanga, in Rhodesia, he had his own farm of 100,000 acres to develop, and he built in the Matopos a dam which took four years to complete and irrigated 2000 acres. During these years he spent more time on the veld than ever before, his usual companions being his 'young men' Grimmer, Jourdan, and J. G. Macdonald, and his friend Sir Charles Metcalfe, besides his coloured factotum Tony de la Cruz, and several young native menservants, one of whom was particularly distinguished. On these excursions, says J. G. Macdonald, Rhodes was ' a different being, becoming like a gleeful boy who had just got his school holidays '—it is really noteworthy how often Rhodes's boyishness is alluded to by different writers. There was much badinage out on the veld, and some shooting, but of course no ' loafing.' Rhodes found plenty of business to do wherever he went, and the Midas touch did not fail him just because he happened to be in a remote place. Walking by himself one day on one of his Rhodesian farms, he noticed the cattle jostling to get at a bluish-coloured grass. He watched them and saw that they were eating nothing else, so he brought home an armful and had it sent to a botanist at the Cape. 'Rhodes grass' has now been distributed in various parts of the world, and is a valuable pasture-grass.

The progress of the Cape to Cairo railway was much in his thoughts.[1] Kitchener was endeavouring to carry the Egyptian section south to the borders of Uganda, while Rhodes was, as usual, pushing northwards. He came to London at the beginning of 1899, and he and Beit persuaded the public to subscribe £3,000,000 to extend the railway from Buluwayo to Tanganyika. He then went to Egypt, where he met Kitchener, and discussed irrigation and railways ; crossed to

[1] 'The outer and visible reasons why the Cape to Cairo line is coming into being are simple and obvious enough. The first and dominating cause is the fact that the idea has fascinated the imagination of Mr. Rhodes, and the second and hardly less potent reason is the fact that the Cape and Cairo both begin with the letter C. Possibly this second reason ought to have precedence over the first, for who knows how much of the fascination which has caught Mr. Rhodes's fancy was due to "apt alliteration's artful aid"? If the Cape and Cairo had possessed different initials, the suggestion of a through continental line might never have suggested itself to Mr. Rhodes. But the notion of linking the two places, each of which commenced with the same capital letter, "caught on," and the gigantic enterprise is already making progress from the realm of the imagination into the domain of accomplished fact.'—From an article by W. T. Stead in the *Windsor Magazine* for September 1899.

Rome for a talk with Jameson ; and went on to Berlin to see the Kaiser, with whom he found time for a ' genial interchange of chaff ' about the telegram of 1896. ' I was a naughty boy,' he explained, ' and you tried to whip me. Now my people were quite ready to whip me for being a naughty boy, but directly *you* did it, they said, " No, if this is anybody's business, it is ours." The result was that Your Majesty got yourself very much disliked by the English people, and I never got whipped at all.' He found Wilhelm ' a big man, a broad-minded man '—presumably because that monarch did not oppose the taking of his telegraph line through German East Africa. Leopold II., whom he also found time to visit, was much less amenable, and after an interview with him, Rhodes is said to have ' hissed ' in the nearest available English ear, ' Satan ! I tell you that man is Satan ! '

On his return to England he and Kitchener were given honorary degrees at Oxford, although there had been some opposition to this proceeding. When he was standing before the Vice-Chancellor in the Sheldonian, and shoulder to shoulder with Kitchener, a woman was heard to remark, ' Oh, don't they just look like two great pillars of the Empire ! '

XVI

BEFORE visiting Egypt he had received a letter from a certain Princess Catherine Radziwill, whom he had once met at a dinner, saying that she had inherited £150,000, and asking his advice as to how she should invest it. He replied that he never gave advice of that sort, and in the same breath suggested that she should buy Mashonaland Railway debentures. This was by no means the last he heard of her. During that early summer of 1899 business obliged him to put off again and again the date of his departure to Africa, and again and again an excitable middle-aged woman called at the offices of the shipping company to find out exactly when Mr. Rhodes was sailing. Mr. Rhodes managed to sail at last on the 18th June.

'Oh, is she here?' he said, when he heard that she was on board. 'I wonder what takes her to South Africa?' He did not have to wonder long, for on the very first evening of the voyage the Princess 'glided into the saloon.' Fat and forty-seven, with black hair and lively dark eyes, she could not, although ' gorgeously gowned and got up to captivate,' have been called either handsome or pretty. However, tripping along lightly, her silk train rustling, she made a bee-line for Rhodes's table. When she met his glance, she appeared overcome with surprise, and as if to atone for the aplomb of her arrival, made a great show of timidity and coyness, slipping diffidently into an empty chair at the same table, which she kept for the rest of the voyage. Feeling that she had taken the first step in the conquest she had planned, she began to talk brightly on every subject that cropped up.

She was temperamental, she was Russian, and therefore (one might almost say) garrulous in several languages. The very reason for her going to Africa was advanced with more than eloquence. Lowering her voice dramatically, she explained that her husband was a brute, a monster of cruelty, but that in Russia the machinery of divorce was slow and complicated, and that while it was grinding out her freedom she wanted to go right away and try and forget. ' She spoke like a martyr sometimes, with a soft, trembling, hesitating voice full of pathos and sadness,' so that the most innocent of Rhodes's attendants felt the blood stirring in his veins, and felt also ' as if he would kill the brutal Prince Radziwill if ever he met him.'

She has been called ' a woman of the baleful and desolating order.' To-day we should be tempted to call her, more vulgarly, a gold-digger. She recognised in Rhodes a Golconda and Eldorado combined, and set herself to woo him with more energy than skill. It was noticed that while she opposed others in argument and became quite excited, she nearly always agreed with whatever Rhodes said. Like the patter of a conjurer, such a stream of brilliant conversation poured from her lips that the hearer, or victim, almost forgot to wonder whether she had anything up her sleeve. She held him fascinated, embarrassed, and bewildered by turns. It required no great subtlety to discern the nature of Rhodes's ' dreams,' and she soon revealed herself to him as a raging Imperialist. She meant to start a paper, she said, to explain the aims and glory of the British Empire. As if this was not enough of an appeal in itself, she began to complain of her heart, ' rolled her eyes and sighed and panted for breath in a most distressing way,' and once, sitting beside Rhodes on deck, she fainted into his arms. He stood there in the utmost confusion, propping her up like a sack of potatoes until help arrived.

This swoon, besides being quite out of fashion (the 'New Woman' was already on the warpath), was a tactical error, and everybody noticed that Rhodes carefully avoided being left alone with the Princess after that. However, before the voyage was over, he gave her a general invitation to lunch at Groote Schuur whenever she felt like it, and offered her the use of his horses to ride. Here again she was clumsy. She took the fullest advantage of his offer, and kept on coming to lunch and dinner. She insisted on being shown over the house by Rhodes himself, and tried to get him alone in a bedroom, but each time he was just too quick for her, having ordered a secretary beforehand to stand by and protect him. She began to bore him, to tire him, and to arouse his suspicions, for she was always talking about politics—most foreign women, he explained to a secretary, are disposed to intrigue.

She still seasoned her political causeries with coyness, and once turned the conversation to chivalry and the Middle Ages, quoting the lines:

'Mon âme à Dieu,
Mon bras au roi,
Mon cœur aux dames,
L'honneur à moi!'

147

' Ah yes ! ' Rhodes replied. ' In those days one could still think about such things.' And that, she said later, proved to her that he had ' no comprehension of the real sense of the beautiful words.' So she tried politics again. Whereupon he lost his temper and cried, ' Leave me alone ! ' But she had no intention of leaving him alone, and began to lay deep schemes.

Meanwhile the South African War was imminent. Rhodes, whose influence had done so much to bring it about, did not foresee it. ' Nothing will make Kruger fire a shot,' he said cocksurely. ' The notion of the Transvaal being able to trouble Great Britain at all seriously is too ridiculous . . . there is not the slightest chance of war.' But Kruger had not forgotten the Kaiser's telegram, and no doubt counted on German support. Besides, he undoubtedly felt, and knew that there were people all over the world who felt with him, that the Transvaal Republic had a right to an existence independent of England.

At the outbreak of the war, Rhodes went to Kimberley, to help to defend his diamond mines. The inability to see any point of view but his own had been growing upon him for some time. It had made him overbearing and intolerant, rude at times even to guests at his own table, and generally difficult to have to do with. He had so long been used to regarding himself, not without cause, as an almighty company-builder and empire-promoter that he had lost most of any faculty he might have had before of self-criticism. But the arrogance of a man who has been poisoned by power is sometimes more clearly to be understood when, like Rhodes, he is the victim of disease : there was surely a connection here between the swollen heart and the swollen head. The destiny of nations must often have been swayed by the faulty blood-pressure of dictators.

Rhodes now saw himself as the centre of Kimberley, and Kimberley as the centre of the war, though of course it was nothing of the kind. He pestered the English generals with messages demanding that the town should be relieved as a necessary first step towards victory. And Colonel Kekewich, who was in command of the town itself, scarcely had his task eased by the disobedience to authority of its leading citizen, who in some ways made a perfect nuisance of himself. In others Rhodes was most useful. He organised some mounted volunteers and other means of defence ; he opened a soup kitchen and sent some grapes to the hospital. He also encouraged the manufacture of a gun called 'Long Cecil,' of which the shells were inscribed *With compts. C. J. R.* But on the whole he seems to have done no more and no less than any capable organiser, possessed of local omnipotence, would have done in the circumstances.

In October 1900, after Roberts had reached Pretoria, Rhodes made a speech at Cape Town to a body of local jingoes. He did not bring them quite what they expected. 'You think you have beaten the Dutch,' he said, ' but it is not so. The Dutch are not beaten ; what is beaten is Krugerism, a corrupt and evil government, no more Dutch in essence than English. No ! The Dutch are as vigorous and unconquered to-day as they have ever been ; the country is still as much theirs as it is yours, and you will have to live and work with them hereafter as in the past. . . . Let there be no vaunting words, no vulgar triumph over your Dutch neighbours ; make them feel that the bitterness is past.'

These remarks reveal both Rhodes's common sense and his lack of real vision. The effort to separate ' Krugerism ' from the nation that evolved it is vain, for Kruger, though an odd and obstinate and in some ways an

ignorant old man, was, in his very oddness
and obstinacy and ignorance, quintessentially
Dutch—that was his strength. In the later
sentences of this speech there is a show of
magnanimity, but was it not a magnanimity
based firmly on the principle that civil strife
is no aid to commerce? The speech offers
no evidence that Rhodes was not blind to the
fact that the Dutch, by their very nature, were
destined to come sooner or later into the pre-
dominance which they regarded as their
right. 'The racehorse is swifter than the
ox,' Kruger had said. But the ox is patient.

It needed Olive Schreiner, that brilliant
woman born and bred in the country, to esti-
mate the real character of the Dutch. 'Virile,
resolute, passionate,' she called them, ' with a
passion hid far below the surface, they are at
once the gentlest and the most determined
of peoples. Under the roughest exterior of
the up-country Boer lies a nature strangely
sensitive and conscious of a personal dignity
—a people who never forget a kindness and
do not easily forget a wrong.' She might have
added that they have often shown themselves,
like the English, capable of cruelty, cupidity
and cunning. But it was Rhodes's inability to
allow for that ' personal dignity ' in others

that half-blinded him to the future of the Dutch, just as the persistent inability of the whites in South Africa to allow for the personal dignity of the blacks still blinds them to the fact that the latter, yes, they too, may sooner or later come into their own.

When someone suggested to him that it was an ' awful pity ' that the war had ever broken out, Rhodes denied it and said, ' It is a good thing. It has made Englishmen respect Dutchmen and made them respect one another.' Was he right ? Is human nature really so base that only mutual murder on a large scale can help to conjure up a little mutual respect between races ? History scarcely seems to show that war leads to what is called ' a better understanding ' ; and as for peace, that seems to lead to war.

At the time when Rhodes made his speech Princess Radziwill was in Cape Town preparing to publish her Imperialist review, which was to be called *Greater Britain*. She had meanwhile produced a ' reply ' to Olive Schreiner's *Trooper Peter Halkett*, in which Rhodes was described as a Creator, and, accurately enough, as one who ' worked for that flag, and, what is more, made others work for it '—the flag which he had described

as a 'commercial asset.' But in her efforts
to get hold of Rhodes she was slightly over-
reaching herself. She sent him a typewritten
account of an interview that she said she had
had with Lord Salisbury. In it the latter was
made to praise Rhodes very highly. The
document was a palpable fake, as Rhodes soon
discovered by making the most simple en-
quiries. But the lady was by now in full gallop,
and no power on earth could stop her. Almost
everybody she met she told 'in confidence'
that she was Rhodes's mistress ; that he used
to visit her alone at night at her hotel ; that
she was secretly engaged to him ; and that she
had already selected her own rooms at Groote
Schuur. But alas, the visits, the betrothal,
the boudoir and the bed, all belonged to the
world of her fancies. So, with all the frenzy
of an over-ambitious, middle-aged and hopelessly frustrated Russian man-eater, she took
to forgery. She forged a diary of a visit to
Hatfield, she forged letters and cables from
London, and finally she forged in Rhodes's
name a number of bills of exchange for very
considerable sums of money.

When Rhodes went back to England those
who knew him well were shocked at his
appearance. He was bloated and ' livid with

a purple tinge in his face.' He was, in fact, approaching his last days. He travelled about in Italy, Egypt and Scotland, in a restless search for health, and was thinking of going to live at Dalham, a house he had bought in Suffolk, when news came from the Cape that the searchlight of the law had at last fallen upon the Princess Radziwill. If Rhodes had ever had any illusions about her, he had none left now, and he wanted to make it quite clear at the Cape that his relationship with her had borne little resemblance to what she had claimed, and that gossip must be silenced. True to his excellent policy of appearing in person where there were difficulties to be settled, and anxious, perhaps, to ' teach her a lesson,' he decided to go to Africa and give evidence against her. And that, of course, meant leaving England, which he was scarcely fit to do.

XVII

In January 1902 he set out, sick and cross, on this last voyage to Africa. Many weeks of his life had been spent on voyages. In the course of them chess was played, there were drinks and talks about money and politics, there were those intrigues and personalities which especially flourish on ocean liners. And these voyages had not been without a touch of fantasy. During one of them an obscure young woman had appeared at the customary fancy-dress ball in a costume representing 'Cape to Cairo,' with a picture of Table Mountain and Table Bay in water-colours at the bottom, and pictures representing the chief towns on the way to Cairo all the way up the skirt, all joined together with a string of tele-graph poles and wire in black, while on her head was a fez and crescent, one breast being covered with a portrait of Kitchener and the other with a portrait of Rhodes himself. But perhaps to some solitary passenger leaning on the rails, oceans of melancholy and firmaments of indifference would seem to extend on all sides a promise of oblivion. Thus poor Barney Barnato, the victim of a persecution mania, finding no solace in bottles, had thrown himself overboard and ' ended it all.'

Rhodes had usually carried to sea a cow, a crate of hens, and his own champagne and kümmel. On this last voyage there was in addition a third-class cabin crammed with delicacies from Messrs. Fortnum & Mason. But although the *Briton* was a floating cornucopia, the ' Old Man ' was troubled by his nerves. He couldn't settle down to chess, and played bridge instead. When the game went against him, as it often did, he rose abruptly from the table and went to bed. Was this the behaviour of a sportsman, of a gentleman ? It was very hot, and alcohol made him no cooler. One night he went to sleep on a writing-table instead of in his bunk, rolled off it, injured his shoulder and knee, and nearly broke his nose. He also caught a chill, which affected his heart badly.

On arriving at the Cape he went straight to his cottage at Muizenberg, and the very next day had to give evidence in the action brought for recovery on the bills. He denied that they bore his signature, and the verdict was given in his favour. Princess Radziwill, however, had already begun an action of her own against him. It was very hot, and he was a sick man, and he began to speak of returning to England, but he had to come to court again to give evidence against the Princess, and the effort made him weaker. The Princess was not lucky in law. In fact, she was in the end sentenced to eighteen months' hard labour. After which the eccentric creature began another action against the Rhodes Trustees for £400,000 damages. In later life, indefatigable as ever, she was to write some sour and ineffectual pages about her former idol.

The heat was intense at the Cape that summer, and Rhodes hurried back in his 12-14 h.p. Wolseley to meet the Muizenberg breeze. But there was no breeze. He took to his bed. He was ill, he was hot, and spoke continually of wanting to return to England. An extra window was knocked through the wall of the cottage, and little groups of 'loafers' collected and kept staring in at the sweating invalid. Princess Radziwill, not yet in gaol, also tried to get a peep at him, but all the defences of the cottage had been mustered to deny her entrance, and she went away

in a huff. Holes were cut in the ceiling, above
which stood tins full of ice, and a punkah was
kept moving day and night over the sick man's
head. His legs became dropsical, and a
cylinder of oxygen appeared at his bedside.
Then Jack Grimmer arrived, and Rhodes
would hardly allow him out of his sight. Dr.
Jameson was tirelessly attentive, Queen Alex-
andra sent him a message of sympathy, and
the patient managed to eat the best part of a
guinea-fowl and to drink a bottle of hock.
But nothing could save him now. His head
sank forward on his breast, and he was heard
to murmur those dreadfully appropriate last
words, ' So little done, so much to do.' Soon
afterwards he actually sang, in a far-away voice
and as if to himself, a snatch of a song that
nobody recognised. And before long he was
dead. It was the afternoon of the 26th March
1902.

' Up to that moment,' says one of his secretaries, ' I had succeeded in suppressing my
tears, but as I stood there in the lonely, simple
room, and realised for the first time that I
should never see his genial smile or his beautiful clear blue eyes light up, or hear his kind
and friendly voice again, I could no longer
restrain myself, and I felt the warm drops

trickle down my cheeks.' These are, to say the least, the accents of a faithful servant on losing a generous master, and that sentence is probably the most heartfelt tribute ever paid to Rhodes in print. That he could inspire it will seem to some people a more graceful achievement than some of those vast and ruthless schemes to which his life was given up.

' Now the labourer's task is o'er,' they sang over his coffin, for whatever he had or had not been, it was quite plain to everybody that he had not been a ' loafer.' By his own rather sentimental wish he was buried, as is well known, in Rhodesia, in a hole in the top of a hill.

XVIII

As a character put faithfully into a novel,
Rhodes might impress but would no doubt
fail to ' convince ' the reviewers. They would
complain that a character must develop, and
it is perhaps difficult to find traces of real
development in Rhodes's nature. His greatness lies in his being so important and effective
an instrument of destiny. He was aware of
this himself, and of the unconscious origin
of his conscious purpose. Speaking of his
' dreams,' he once said in a speech, ' I do not
claim any credit—I simply say that they were
the thoughts that came to me—that is all.
You may discover the microbe of the rinderpest, but I defy you ever to find the microbe
of the human imagination. You do not know
where it comes from, but it comes and the
thoughts come, and you are moved as a human
atom to carry out those thoughts.' His abilities when quite a young man do not seem to
have been inferior to his later powers, though
naturally his opportunities were fewer. His

judgment of his fellow-men did not improve ;
he made no advance in culture or statesman-
ship ; after all his experience of the Dutch
he understood them so little that, as we have
seen, he thought the Boer War an impossi-
bility ; his boyish ' dreams ' were modified
by necessity and not by wisdom ; and he
never underwent that particular kind of education so usefully provided for some men by a
close association with a mature woman of the
world who knows how to manage her man
and can help him to steer his best course.
Indeed, after the death of his mother when he
was twenty, the civilising influence of women
was mostly absent from his life. It was not
Rhodes that grew, but his bank balance, his
activities, and his power, and in many respects
he always remained what one of his chief
intimates considered him—' a great baby.'

' That is my dream,' he said, pointing to the
map of Africa, ' all red ! ' Thinking always
too much in terms of land and money, he
made too little allowance for the powers of
racial and personal sentiment, and had few
scruples about interference with other people
in order to advance his own interests. He
imagined that every man ' has his price,' and
once told General Gordon that if one has

ideas, one cannot carry them out without
wealth to back them. ' I have therefore
tried,' he said, ' to combine the commercial
with the imaginative.' Imaginative ! To
what extraordinary uses words are sometimes
put ! To be far-seeing in business, on however
large a scale, is scarcely the equivalent of
being ' imaginative,' but it is not unusual for
successful capitalists to flatter themselves or
be flattered in this way. We have been told,
in their several heydays, that Messrs. Ford,
Bata and Kreuger were ' imaginative,' and
no doubt Sir Basil Zaharoff was ' imaginative '
when, in June 1917, he used his influence to
urge that the Great War should be continued
' *jusqu'au bout*.' As for Rhodes, ' it is the vice
of a vulgar mind,' says a character in *Howard's
End*, ' to be thrilled by bigness, to think that
a thousand square miles are a thousand times
more wonderful than one square mile, and
that a million square miles are almost the
same as heaven. That is not imagination.
No, it kills it.'

Mr. Basil Williams seeks to justify Rhodes's
creed on the grounds of his deep sense of
public duty, his tenacity of purpose, and,
above all, on his ' underlying sympathy and
desire for co-operation even with opponents,

without which it was meaningless.' To those at all sceptically inclined, it will seem that a sense of public duty so closely allied with a progressive personal aggrandisement may possibly be suspect ; that the merit of perseverance is in proportion to the merits of the object in view ; that sympathy is not best expressed with double-dealing and dynamite ; and that the desire to win opponents over to one's side for the furtherance of one's own aims is by no means uncommon among the ambitious.

Every day, with Rhodes, was Empire Day. Like his friend Rudyard Kipling, he seems to have held the fanciful belief that the British are a chosen race, and that what they do and think is right. In order to help to enrich and consolidate the race, he wished to promote an Imperial zollverein. But since Rhodes's time the Empire has ceased to exist —it has long been known, even officially, as a Commonwealth of Nations. And as for ' Empire Free Trade,' are we to believe that any business person will ever prefer to sell sixpennyworth of goods to Australia rather than a shilling's worth to some sounder country ? *Britannia rules the waves* is still sung, but of course Britannia does nothing of the

163

kind, and can scarcely, with her hungry millions, be said to be perfect in ruling herself.

Rhodes undoubtedly foreshadowed, though he was not the first to propose, the Union of South Africa which took place in 1910. 'A speculator's dream,' said Olive Schreiner, who believed in what she called the value of human varieties ; ' a speculator's dream of breaking down all the interstatal lines which have stood out as so many small ramparts behind which freedom could hide and which broke into parts the wave of capitalist aggression as it swept on.' But in any case Rhodesia has never entered the Union, and there is already a movement in Natal in favour of secession from it. The Union is to-day in all but name an Afrikander republic—its government is Dutch, its representatives abroad are Dutch, its civil service is Dutch, its defence and police forces are Dutch, and its flag is not the Union Jack. The ' imaginative ' Rhodes reckoned without that sturdy independence which is inherent in the Dutch character. But let us remember that the commercial Rhodes obtained for his country dominions ' larger than Spain, France and the former German Empire put together.' It is no wonder that he was arrogant. ' Whenever I took a country,' he boasted, ' I simply said to the Queen, " I have taken that : you must put your flag over it." ' Arrogance led to megalomania. ' I would annex the planets if I could,' he said to Stead, ' *I often think of that.*' And so sure was he of the rightness of his life, that he vaingloriously declared his readiness to ' have it out with Almighty God ' —which is either blasphemy or nonsense, or both, and is interesting to compare with Kruger's ' I shall have to appear before Him, and when I think of that, my heart fails me, and I can only pray.'

It is beyond question that the ideas which Rhodes and many others stood for helped to make not only the Boer War but the Great War possible. Those ideas, infallible as they may have seemed yesterday, are widely questioned to-day. A character in a recent novel by Henri Barbusse names property and patriotism as two of the most frightful manifestations of tradition, and goes on to say that ' every word of hatred and revolt against militarism, every insult to the flag, every anti-patriotic appeal has its sources in beauty and the ideal.' The fate which threatens mankind as the result of indiscriminate capitalism, ' Christianity,' and scientific warfare is now clear, and in view of it we may hope for the modi-

fication of certain beliefs that have been long
and firmly held, beliefs in the service of which
Rhodes spent his life. We cannot sit in judgment ; being human, we too are probably
wrong, and it is possible to be quite as bigoted
in vainly anticipating an enlightened system
under, let us say, the red flag or no flag at all
as under the Union Jack. We only know that
we are just as much the children of one age
as Rhodes was the child of another ; we know
too that there have been men comparable to
Rhodes in every age ; but, in the words of the
new president of the British Association, ' accepted predilections as to national sovereignty
have to be abandoned if the world is to keep
the peace and allow civilisation to survive.'
Rhodes honestly believed that he was working
for civilisation, but some people in his own day
and many more in ours could argue that he
was in the long run working against it. He
behaved as if he lived in a world free from
uncertainties, and that is in any age characteristic of the man of action, who seems to be as
necessary to the life we know as the man of
imagination. Rhodes is remembered as one of
the major prophets of capitalist Imperialism,
and whether we revere or merely wonder at his
phenomenal activities, we are bound to remem-

ber him as a most typical representative of an age and country swollen with wealth, blinded by pride, and headed for disaster.

By his last will he left a fortune of several million pounds. He left Groote Schuur as a residence for the Prime Minister of a federated South Africa ; Dalham, his English estate, to his family, with a direction against any ' loafer ' inheriting it ; £100,000 to Oriel College ; his vast estates of more than 200,000 acres in Rhodesia were left in trust for the settlers there ; and land was given for a Rhodesian University. Most interesting of all was his provision for 160 Scholarships to be founded at Oxford, of a value of £300 each, to be held by two students from every state of the U.S.A., and three from each of eighteen British colonies. Fifteen other Scholarships of the value of £250 each were reserved for German students, to be chosen by the so much admired Kaiser Wilhelm II. The Rhodes Scholar was to be chosen for—

' (i) his literary and scholastic attainments ;
(ii) his fondness of and success in manly outdoor sports such as cricket, football and the like ;
(iii) his qualities of manhood, truth, courage, devotion to duty, sympathy for

the protection of the weak, kindliness, unselfishness and fellowship ; and

(iv)   his exhibition during school days of moral force of character and of instincts to lead and to take an interest in his schoolmates, for those latter attributes will be likely in after-life to guide him to esteem the performance of public duty as his highest aim.'

What could be more admirable or more rare than a man with a really healthy body, a truly alert mind, and a genuinely kind heart ? This ideal ' scholar ' of Rhodes's, however, this successful footballer and kindly *littérateur*, this dutiful hero and moral exhibitionist, this cricketing paragon of muscular Christianity, has none of the splendour of some Greek or Renaissance imagining, but a close relationship to some common types of upper middle-class Victorian manhood, the server of Mammon in the name of God, or the painfully earnest and misguided missionary. He is a day-dream left over from what D. H. Lawrence has called ' the century that tried to destroy humanity, that great century of lies which, thank God, we are drifting away from.' Although Rhodes specifically stated that race and creed should be no bar in the selection of his ' scholars,' he evidently aimed at the production of a ' Christian gentleman ' with no nonsense about him. Human beings have a remarkable faculty for becoming what they want to become, and then giving it a fine name ; the truth is, that the sport-loving, materialistic Puritan who regards himself as a Christian gentleman is only too often neither Christian nor gentle, but just aggressively stupid. His exhibition of moral force and attention to public duty are apt to blind him to the fact that, while ' lofty idealism ' and indiscriminate philanthropy may look very well in the world, charity begins at home.

The English, it has been asked—are they human ? Was Rhodes human ? It is arguable that many of the less agreeably human activities of the English, and also of the Scotch—a race extraordinarily well represented in the annals of African colonisation —are traceable to the fear that there is something shameful and unmanly in gentleness, gaiety and sensuality, and that this fear leads to a kind of emotional stricture which sometimes starves and warps us, and makes us dour, violent, or even perverted in our behaviour. And it seems to me that the ideal Rhodes Scholar would develop into a cold and truculent sahib with a thorough knowledge of ball-games and a complete ignorance of the real arts of living. He would, in fact, be slightly inhuman.

Surely in describing his proposed ' scholars ' Rhodes revealed not the ' vision ' which has been claimed for him, but an unawareness of the future, and of the kind of qualifications a man needs to grapple with the complexities of life in this first half of the twentieth century. He might well have arranged for each of these young men to be taught a trade, and to learn something of science, as well as of the workings of the human mind and body. If he meant to train a sort of Nazis to enforce certain fixed ideas in wide areas, he should have left some stricter foundation, some college, for the purpose. But if he meant to produce men to influence the thought of their age, he should have known better than to expect that those ' all-round ' young men, who are to be found in every school and university, would be able to fulfil his purpose. As a rule, they neither make history nor do they even make much of their opportunities. As for subsidising sympathy, kindliness, etc., the idea is childish—' Be a good boy and you shall have a nice scholarship.'

What of the Rhodes Scholar in South Africa? Let us quote an authority on that country, Mr. Leonard Barnes : ' The impression left on the Rhodes Scholar by his European experiences generally, and by his experience of Oxford in particular, is always either negligible or profound, according to the character of his sensibility. When it is negligible, the young man comes home, and, blending naturally with his background, never emerges from obscurity. When it is profound, he feels himself so fundamentally at odds with the uncouthness and spiritual waste of South African life in many of its political, economic and social aspects that he cannot without hypocrisy share it, except in a superficial sense.' From which we may conclude that in the rare cases where his education makes a profound impression on a Rhodes Scholar there is just a chance that he may have enough gumption to ' perform ' the ' public duty ' of showing up the ' uncouthness and spiritual waste ' of his country. And that is probably the best justification of the Rhodes Scholarships as far as South Africa is concerned.

An American Rhodes Scholar has said that

the tendency with his fellows there is to enter academic rather than political life, and that they are apt to bring back with them from Oxford not a raging thirst for universal Nordic domination, or whatever else it was that Rhodes intended them to acquire, but just a touch of polite scepticism.

BIBLIOGRAPHICAL NOTE

RHODES was so widely concerned in the life of his time, and so plainly a figure in the world as well as in South Africa, that the amount of printed matter relating to him is by no means small. Besides, it is only thirty years since he died, and there are many living who remember him in the flesh, though no doubt few fresh facts will be brought to light. The best, most solid and comprehensive book about him, and one perhaps well known to that rather mythical person, the general reader, is the biography by Mr. Basil Williams (Constable, 1921), which is based on a great variety of materials, and furnished with a bibliography most useful to the specialist. Able as it is, it may well be found too tolerant and at moments just a trifle rhapsodic; but at present it must be regarded as the standard life, though it may be argued that some time must pass before Rhodes can be seen in a proper historical perspective. I have made a number of references to and quotations from Mr. Williams.

Sir Lewis Michell's biography, the two books by the private secretaries, Jourdan and Le Sueur (who let some instructive cats out of the bag), W. T. Stead's annotated reprint of the will, the collection of speeches by Vindex with their biassed commentary, Ian D. Colvin's life of Jameson, Vere

Stent's, Howard Hensman's, and J. G. Macdonald's more or less personal records, Sir Percy Fitzpatrick's *The Transvaal from Within*, F. J. Dormer's *Vengeance as a Policy in Afrikanderland*, and H. R. Fox-Bourne's lucid pamphlet *Matabeleland and the Chartered Company*—these are but a few of the essential foundations of a study of Rhodes. English and South African newspapers and governmental publications of the period are, of course, full of material, and points are furnished by numerous books of travel, memoirs, etc. Most writers on Rhodes's policy seem almost as little concerned to consider the point of view of the Dutch, the Germans, and the Portuguese as that of the natives. Some, again, take care not to mention Olive Schreiner and her books. Reference may well be made to the *Life* and *Letters* produced by her widower, as well as to her own writings, especially *Thoughts on South Africa* and *Trooper Peter Halkett of Mashonaland*. The existence of such works as Leonard Woolf's *Empire and Commerce in Africa*, Leonard Barnes's *Caliban in Africa* and *The Next Boer War*, and Lord Olivier's *The Anatomy of African Misery* serve as a reminder that there are level-headed men with colonial, political and literary experience who actually have doubts about the seemliness of ' scrambling ' for other people's countries, and clear ideas about the nature and effects of the colour bar.

Sources consulted for the present sketch range from the evidence given before the Select Committees on the Raid to *The Choir Invisible*, from Kruger's *Memoirs* to Mackenzie's long-winded *Austral Africa*, from the lucubrations of the redoubtable Radziwill to conversations with a man who actually took part in the Raid. If I have quoted from other sources than those already mentioned, my excuse must be that the scope of this series does not allow of the use of detailed footnotes. I apologise for omissions and shortcomings, and make due acknowledgment of my debt to the efforts of many previous writers and to the publishers of those efforts. And I must not forget to thank those who have given me personally the benefit of their experience and advice.

INDEX

INDEX